LEFT-SIDE LIE

Cider Spoon Stories
Austin, Texas
www.ciderspoonstories.com

Cover design by Summer Stark for Summer Stark Design
Editing and book design by Jessica Bross
Manufactured in the United States of America

9 8 7 6 5 4 3 2 1

for my son
whose heart is full of goodness
and whose strength keeps me balanced and grounded

CONTENTS

MAY 2017

In the peaceful quiet over my morning cup of coffee, a reflection of pain, real and raw, stared back at me from my cup. All I wanted to do was pick up the phone and reach out to family and friends, to analyze the preposterous events that had lately unfolded in my life. Talking through them was how I'd always made sense of my wounds; once spoken aloud, they (usually) started to heal. However, I knew I could only subject my loved ones to a limited amount of personal despair before I wore out my welcome and became the phone call they didn't want to answer.

Loathe to cross that thin line, and at the suggestion of my faith-based therapist, I turned to journaling instead. Slowly, sleepless nights and distracted days became words on paper, words became paragraphs, paragraphs became pages, and the pages turned into chapters. Three years later, I had a book—a chronicle of my recovery from being married to a criminal narcissist.

*

Even with all the evidence staring me in the face—damning photos and shocking video clips, unbelievable statements from lawyers and private investigators—my reality was at times difficult to digest. Early journal entries reflected that. They skipped and meandered and doubled-back, jumping in time as new revelations came to light. The tense alternated between present and past depending on how close to or removed from a given subject or event I felt. Some pages were tear-stained. Still, there remained a clear through-line: the story of a heart bruised by years of lies and deception. I only told it to my journal back then because I couldn't tell anyone else. Now, I only share it because it's over. The end has come in the form of a federal judgment for multiple counts of government fraud. My former husband has been stopped and is facing the consequences as I type.

Full disclosure: I'm not a writer or a behavioral expert. My only qualification for writing about narcissism is integrating everything I've learned about the patterns of this destructive personality disorder with my years of experience as a victim. In that sense, it's something almost any victim of a narcissist could do, since the traits of narcissism are consistent (albeit with differing levels of severity) across the board. Broadly speaking, these skirt outside the understanding of moral people and can have dire, long-lasting impacts on unsuspecting targets. If you haven't lived in the midst of narcissism, a victim's account may seem to you like a made-up story, a *Dateline* episode, or a *Lifetime* movie. But narcissism is a diagnosable mental disorder that causes collateral damage and leaves behind real casualties. Luckily, I was able to get justice and closure through the federal court system. Not everyone is so fortunate.

My former husband is a brilliant conman and superior manipulator. He not only perpetrated many layers of domestic fraud against me, but he also believed he could outsmart several agencies within the federal government. All along, I thought I had the perfect husband, handsome, sweet, and caring. That was until I stumbled upon the first sign of Ty's elaborate scam, a single snowflake in what would become an avalanche of lies and deceit. Once that first flake hit the ground, it was like a clown car had pulled up in the driveway, horn honking and clowns popping out from every door and window. There were erotic full-service massage parlors, secret mountains of debt, and faked disabilities so devastating they left my head spinning. Worse, though, was what Ty stole—and I don't mean the diamonds and money he took from me, though he took those, too. Rather, he stole resources and, most despicably, valor from fellow soldiers who deserved it far more than he did, men and women who had actually made the sacrifices about which retired Army officer Ty bragged. It was a layer cake of disability, healthcare, and wire fraud decorated with the garbage icings of felony theft and military misrepresentation. It looked so pretty from the outside, I never questioned what he was feeding me, not even—though I should have, wish I would have!—on the day we said "I do."

Sadly for my former husband, he misjudged my core belief system and the strength of my foundation in God, family, and friends. He was likewise naïve to the power of the federal justice system and dedicated government law enforcement agents. When Ty was stricken with full left-side paralysis shortly after we married, I, like everyone who knew Ty, bought the story hook, line, and sinker. He was an upstanding and respectable citizen, after all, practically *king* (as an honorably discharged veteran) of our small conservative Texas town. No one, including me or his friends or Ty's sons, knew for two years that he was fully functional and could really walk. Like a school child playing sick to get attention and evade responsibilities, my husband was playing paralyzed for the same reasons. Disabled veterans are heroes. They elicit sympathy. They're entitled to benefits—as well they should be! But Ty's need for sympathy was sociopathic, his hero status painstakingly constructed to conjure maximum personal reward and jaw-dropping financial gain. He deserves an Oscar for what he pulled off. But he deserves, too, to pay the price, which came due once hidden surveillance made clear and federal investigators confirmed what I'd come to suspect. Heck, maybe I deserve an Oscar also, since throughout the investigation I had to play stupid—not paralyzed, but stupid, so he wouldn't get wise. I was forced to become a con to con a con. Unlike Ty, I didn't like it, and if the whole experience taught me anything, it's that no one can escape the truth. Like cream, it always rises to the top.

After Ty's game was exposed, he left behind massive amounts of emotional and financial wreckage. Within days of me abruptly leaving him, he began grooming a new victim, dropping the bread-crumbs that would mark a new trail of lies and deceit. It doesn't matter to Ty that he's been held liable in a federal court. Within the confines of his own mind, he (still) believes he is above the law, is confident his wrongs are beyond prosecution. Any time he's confronted, he makes plausible excuses for every unlawful act he's committed and deftly explains away his behavior as someone else's fault—while in reality, his actions were always intentional, mas-terminded for emotional control and financial gain. That he also received an abundance of sympathetic attention for his fabricated handicap was the cherry on top feeding his narcissistic ego.

As the ex-wife of a clinical narcissist and federal criminal, my hope is to reach anyone who may unknowingly be trapped in the early stages of this unrelenting and camouflaged behavioral dis-order. If my story triggers thoughts of suspicion in your past or present relationships, I urge you to educate yourself on the charac-teristics of Narcissistic Personality Disorder (NPD) and Factitious Disorder,[1] more commonly known as Munchausen Syndrome.[2]

---

1   "Factitious Disorder." Mayo Clinic. https://www.mayoclinic.org/dis-eases-conditions/factitious-disorder/symptoms-causes/syc-20356028.

2   The name Munchausen Syndrome was coined in 1977 by pediatrician and professor Roy Meadow. He named the disorder after Baron von Munchausen (1720-1797), a German aristocrat known for his extreme hypochondria. Even though two centuries separate Baron von Munchausen and my ex-husband Ty, their patterns of inventing fake medical symptoms and self-inducing illnesses

If your partner currently appears to be what dreams are made of or too good to be true, you may be on a fast-moving train down the destructive track to full consumption. My wish and prayer for you is that you pay attention to the clues and the signs lurking in the shadows. Loving a narcissist is a limited-time offer. The offer expires when you are completely destroyed. The evolution from target to victim moves as swiftly as a golden speeding bullet—and the bleeding it causes is just as slow and sweet. You may not even notice the hemorrhage happening. Don't underestimate this behavioral disorder. It's hard to spot. Narcissism will not jump up and slap you on the face to announce itself. It's charming, calculated … and can devour you over time.

Narcissistic Personality Disorder and Factitious Disorder

My former husband's personality traits tick every box on the checklists of Narcissistic Personality Disorder and Factitious Disorder. This is unsurprising since according to the many medical journals I've read since discovering Ty's secret, individuals with specific personality disorders like NPD are especially susceptible to Factitious Disorder. Until my discovery, I was oblivious to the existence of either behavioral disorder and therefore to the classic signs—namely, an extreme desire for attention coupled with emo-

---

are exactly the same. For more information, see: Olgy, Regis. "Baron Münchhausen and the Syndrome Which Bears His Name: History of an Endearing Personage and of a Strange Mental Disorder." *Vesalius.* June 2002. https://pubmed.ncbi.nlm.nih.gov/12422889/.

tional manipulation, which the narcissist views like a game they play for sport and to gain power over their environment. Here are some additional typical traits:

- **Narcissism**: Superficial charm, grandiose self-worth, pathological lying, acts differently in public than private, distorts facts, twists conversations, changes events to suit their own agenda, gaslighting, emotionally manipulative, irresponsible with money, seeks eroticism, lack of guilt or remorse, creates chaos and drama as a distraction, and has an addictive craving for attention however they can get it. As a result of their bad behavior, they delude themselves into believing their own self-destruction is someone else's fault. They will not take responsibility for their own actions; rather, they make excuses and even tend to believe their own lies.

- **Factitious Disorder**: A personality disorder in which a person repeatedly and deliberately acts as if he or she has a physical or mental illness. Health complications have an unclear or no root cause and are sustaining or incurable. Symptoms tend to change or morph once treatments begin and over time get worse for no apparent reason. Ailments don't respond as expected to treatments. There are often relapses following improvements used as a distraction tactic or as an emotional defense. When these individuals begin to lose control or need attention, they have a health crisis or medical emergency, often inventing new symptoms. Medical conditions will selectively come and go and they can cure themselves with the snap of a finger. They prey on the sympathy of others and have extensive knowledge of hospitals, pharmaceuticals, and medical terminology.

While Ty never studied medicine in any kind of professional capacity, he understood the medical system well. He asked a million questions at every doctor's appointment and learned by "trial and error" what worked and what didn't. He seemed to have a sixth sense for identifying who on staff at each medical facility was naïve or a pushover and would just say "yes" to rush him in and out. Always, Ty was overly nice, almost killing the staff with kindness. The irony is that Ty's extreme kindness was one of the traits that drew me to him initially.

Unlike other diseases, NPD and Factitious Disorder go undetected on the surface and are very hard to diagnose. Factitious Disorder is so rare that few statistics about its prevalence have been made available,[3] while NPD impacts roughly 1-6% of the adult population,[4] with 75% of patients being male.[5] Patients exhibiting

3   Caselli, Ivano. "A Systematic Review on Factitious Disorders: Psychopathology and Diagnostic Classification." *Neuropsychiatry*. 2018. https://www. jneuropsychiatry.org/peer-review/a-systematic-review-on-factitious-disorders-psychopathology-and-diagnostic-classification.pdf

4   Lyon, Lindsay. "Narcissism Epidemic: Why There Are So Many Narcissists Now." *U.S. News and World Report*. 2009. https://health.usnews.com/health-news/family-health/brain-and-behavior/articles/2009/04/21/narcissism-epidemic-why-there-are-so-many-narcissists-now

5   Kacel, Elizabeth L. "Narcissistic Personality Disorder in Clinical Health Psychology Practice: Case Studies of Comorbid Psychological Distress and Life-Limiting Illness." *Behavioral Medicine*. 2017. https://www.ncbi.nlm.

either or both behavioral disorders are architects of emotion, adept at building strong support systems in the form of their victims. However, the ultimate intent is to demolish the structure like a child destroying a Lego house. The challenge is in the construction, but the fun is in the anticipation and control of the destruction.

The Narcissist's Toolbox: Love Bombing, Supply, Gaslighting, and Mirroring

So many people have had an unforgettable encounter with a narcissist and have their own damaging stories to tell that I strongly believe the NPD statistics are under-reported. To date, studies have primarily been conducted at medical facilities or through clinical evaluations of the prison population, not the general public. There are everyday narcissists walking among us posing as chameleons who are not included in these clinical studies or statistical calculations. Unfortunately, the word *narcissist* is overused and thrown around loosely to describe a basic self-centered jerk. Jerks may temporarily act the same as a narcissist on the surface, but internally they are not sociopathic. Their deviant behavior is situational and fleeting, while a narcissist will demonstrate a lifetime of consistent patterns of manipulation and show zero comprehension of empathy or remorse. Moral reasoning as you and I know it simply doesn't apply.

For Ty, these "consistent patterns" were (I later found out) at

---

nih.gov/pmc/articles/PMC5819598/

work in his first marriage, became evident in our marriage, and would repeat in his next relationship. But we can trace them back even further than that—to a childhood where, as the baby of the family, he was made the center of everything. Ty's sales executive father, who was a generation older than Ty's mother (and who had therefore already passed by the time I met Ty), used to put little Ty on his knee as they sang "Me and My Buddy" to a live audience. When I heard this story, I remember thinking to myself that Ty had been used as a sales tactic, little better than a "live puppet," and wondered what these performances had taught him about getting his way. Ty's mother, meanwhile, coddled him, fumbling all over herself to ensure her baby was happy even as an adult man. Never mind that Ty had a sister ten years his senior. Ty was the sun. His family revolved around him, the boy who could do no wrong.

However he became one, there is no question that Ty was and is a narcissist given the techniques he used to deceive me, which are common to all narcissists. Love bombing, supply, gaslighting, and mirroring—we'll break down each of these terms momentarily—are the primary established roots narcissists use to grow and stabilize their trees. Victims become the nutritious soil that sustains and cultivates their fruitful harvest. They fertilize emotional control over their victims by using predatory attraction. Although science tells us that narcissists do not know they are narcissists, and further, that they lack the ability to recognize other narcissists, be forewarned: They are not unique or original in their approach. Patterns and methods are shockingly the same across the board.

- **Love Bombing**: Love bombing is characterized by over-the-top and near-constant displays of attention and affection. These may include flowers, gifts, texts, trips, compliments, and other romantic gestures, as well as long conversations about "our future." The combination of words and deeds makes love bombing a very powerful manipulative tool that is dangerous to the unsuspecting victim as it appears to be genuine. Victims are reeled in by what feels like positive attention—who doesn't like being "put on a pedestal"?—but the narcissist's ultimate end goal is to use them for "supply"—that is, admiration, which in turn boosts the narcissist's ego and self-esteem. All of this makes love bombing without a doubt the most poisonous characteristic as it secures the victim's co-dependency and lays the foundation for future emotional influence.

- **Supply**: Supply to a narcissist is the mental equivalent of a drink to an alcoholic. Narcissists have an addictive desire for admiration, applause, approval, affirmation, love, and compliments delivered either personally or publicly. A narcissist will take supply from unsuspecting victims or create it by provoking drama. If supply is not forthcoming, they will extort it by manufacturing fear and chaos or generating sympathy. Without supply, narcissists crumble and become dysfunctional. It's the reason they are able to turn love on and off in the blink of an eye and move quickly from person to person. Supply is the narcissist's lifeblood.

- **Gaslighting**: Psychological abuse where false information is consistently presented to disorient the victim by making them believe they're losing their mind. Systematic and long-term effects of gaslighting erode the target's perception. They begin to doubt themselves, live in a state of confusion, and no longer trust their own judgment. Gaslighting is a subtle way of brainwashing the victim slowly over time. Gradually, the victim becomes dependent on the abuser for their sense of reality.

- **Mirroring/Positive Mirroring**: Narcissists use mirroring as a means to an end. They will reflect and mimic (or mirror) the behaviors, likes, and dislikes their victims exhibit as a pretense for a genuine relationship. Humans are drawn to other humans who are like them, and narcissists are expert chameleons. When a narcissist emulates a victim's personality, they effectively use the victim's own confidence as a tool. This positioning is so powerful that in turn, the victim sees only what they want to recognize by filtering out the narcissist's undesirable behaviors and identifying strictly with the good (positive mirroring). To a smitten victim made blind by love, the narcissist appears to be perfect in every way. They are like a hypnotic shiny object with no faults. No person from the outside looking in can convince the victim that something about their new partner doesn't seem quite right. It's a futile effort for family or friends to warn a victim that their new relationship really is too good to be true. Words and expression of concern cannot save a victim. They can only be influenced by documented facts and data. A victim must see the proof in the pudding. Without this, they will never believe that their dream partner is a phony manipulating them with fake love and kindness. Suspicious family and friends typically don't have this type of evidence, and more than likely, they are being charmed by the narcissist as well. Narcissists have a crafted and fine-tuned talent for being overly giving, helpful, and charming while engaging the victim's entire social network. They take pride in manipulating their victim's support system. It's a strategic game. The narcissist gets a thrill and feels empowered when a victim and their network believe their lies, fabrications, and manipulations. It's not only a form of control, but a kind of entertainment.

The Textbook Victim

Contrary to popular belief, the typical victim is not naïve or weak. Narcissists don't pursue partners they have to take care of; rather, they seek out individuals who will take care of them. They select independent, self-sufficient, strong partners, people who will be there for them and also feed their egos. (The bigger the challenge, the bigger the ego boost, right?) It takes a special strategy to win over a target like this, so narcissists come on strong in the beginning, providing targets with a fairytale romance like nothing they've ever experienced before. Once a target's been swept firmly off their feet, the narcissist whittles away at their confidence and self-esteem until they begin questioning their own decisions and abilities. The once-independent individual becomes the dependent, confused victim reliant solely on the narcissist to know what's real. And it happens without them realizing. In this way, a narcissist is like a love burglar that prowls through your emotions. Love bombing equates to love theft. The bombs are never genuine and only intended to steal your trust and admiration, so ultimately the narcissist can take your joy, money, and sanity, too. Don't be fooled. They are a predator.

After my fraud discoveries, I learned I was a textbook victim. Raised in a small, rural Texas panhandle farming community, I'm the self-sufficient daughter of two equally hardworking parents who are sun-up-to-sun-down farmers and ranchers. They are conservative Christians and I am, too; both our familial bonds and our faith are strong. Beginning at a very young age, my younger brother and I contributed to the livelihood of the family. This early experience informed my present work ethic and drove me to succeed in college and beyond. After earning a bachelor's degree in Business, I launched my longtime corporate career in Texas's high-tech industry, where I continued to prove myself hardheaded, purpose-driven, and typically impatient. Even now, I weigh personal and business risks heavily—at times, I will admit, over-analyzing them. I have an underlying sense of caution since, as they say, the devil's in the details.

On the flip-side, I'm maternal, empathetic, and generous. My compassion runs deep. It's what led me to become a hospice volunteer after my grandmother's death. I often flinch and feel sorry for roadkill and cannot watch violent or heartbreaking movies because it's too much for me to bear. I also have an adventurous side with an itch for new experiences and world travel, having explored fourteen different countries. When I met Ty, I'd already sampled the history, culture, and food of Germany, Costa Rica, Italy, Vatican City, Switzerland, Austria, England, France, Ireland, the Bahamas, Aruba, Mexico, and Canada and had no intentions of stopping, given that I was in the process of transitioning from single mom to empty-nester. With my college-age son off to higher education, I was alone in the house for the first time. That I paid cash for his college education is one of my proudest accomplishments, other than my son himself. Now that I am well-versed in classic narcissistic behaviors, it all makes sense. I was the perfect prey with plenty of supply and no distractions.

As the days passed, I tried not to be a Monday morning quarterback, but hindsight sometimes got the best of me. Distressing thoughts ran through my head and I would often beat myself up thinking, *Why didn't I catch that? How did I not know?* or *That was so obvious, you stupid idiot!* There were clear signs, patterns, and gut feelings from the very beginning. But instead of questioning the obvious things that made no sense, my positive mirroring was in full force. I followed what I felt were the "wife rules"—loving Ty, caring for him, respecting him, and believing him—and, to my own detriment and demise, dismissed the oddities. Wife rules, it turns out, do not apply when you're in love with and married to a narcissist.

There are no defined words in any dictionary that can describe the earth-shattering feeling I had when I accidentally discovered my disabled husband was fully functional. After years of doctor's appointments, extensive medical tests, and learning to live in a handicapped world, the intense emotion that filled my entire body as our home security cameras caught my disabled husband walking perfectly across the floor was beyond language. Desperate to define this new unexplainable emotion, I searched the internet for days trying to find another spouse who had been through a similar experience. I couldn't find one, making me feel even more isolated and like I was in uncharted territory. *Has anyone else experienced this?* I wondered. *How can I be the only person on planet Earth whose spouse fabricated a handicap and fooled the entire family?*

I wasn't the only person on planet Earth, of course, to have been a narcissist's unwitting victim, but my stories are still rare enough (and shocking enough) to make other people exclaim upon hearing what happened, "You can't *even* make this shit up!" Due to the severe and excessive nature of Ty's deceit, the district judge who heard my case granted my petition for annulment due to fraud[6] less than one hour after the evidence was presented. In the state of Texas, an annulment after two-plus years of marriage is unheard of unless the circumstances are extreme and intentional. Not only did

---

6   Both divorce and annulment result in the end of a marriage. The difference is that in a divorce, a court finds that the marriage was valid and grants the divorce because of something that occurred after the marriage, while in an annulment, a court finds that the marriage was never valid in the first place—something I was entitled to since Ty was already committing fraud on our wedding day. Obtaining an annulment made it as if our marriage never happened, at least in a legal sense.

my case meet both criteria, but the judge expressed to my attorney that mine was the worst case of fraud he'd seen in all his years on the bench. My former husband was allowed twenty-four hours to vacate our home. Our marriage was immediately dissolved as if it had never existed. But, it did exist. My experience was very, very real.

Today, I believe God's hands were guiding every step of the discovery process, as well as the legal team and federal investigators dedicated to exposing the truth. The timing and way in which the chain of events unfolded were not a coincidence but divinely orchestrated. Exposing the truth about the man I loved was the hardest thing I've ever had to do. But it was also the right thing, and as I've learned, it's always the right time to do the right thing … no matter how much it hurts.

And so, my four years with Ty began …

"So do not be afraid of them, for there is nothing concealed that will not be disclosed, or hidden that will not be made known."
—Matthew 10:26

1

....

99% BLUE

"The devil doesn't come dressed in a red cape and pointy horns. He comes as everything you ever wished for." —Tucker Max

From the moment Ty and I met on a Christian dating site, I was certain that he was a miracle brought to me by prayer, perfect timing, and online personality testing algorithms. He had a profile picture that would make any woman stop in her tracks. Because his profile was jaw-dropping, my first impression was that he might be a decoy for the dating site to keep women interested in continuing their pursuit. How could this handsome man be my exact personality type—blue with a 99% match? (I no longer remember what "blue" said about my and Ty's personalities, but the fact that we were the same color and shared nearly 100% of our interests made for better statistics than Vegas odds!) I was convinced the 1% non-match must have been the two-hour driving distance between our cities. He lived in Boerne, Texas, where he was an Army warrant officer in the Signal Core out of San Antonio's Fort Sam Houston, and I lived in Austin. Other than the minor 1% difference, my prayers had been answered and the stars had aligned.

After exchanging several messages online, we graduated to phone calls. Sure enough, Ty was a real person—with a deep, strong voice and wicked sense of humor to boot. He was educated and well-spoken. Conversation flowed easily and naturally, and this despite the fact that Ty was "always on the move" anytime we connected. He had three boys, he told me, aged eighteen, eleven, and eight, and they kept him busy attending their sporting events. That first week, any time we talked it seemed Ty was at or on the way to one of his son's baseball games, which only made me like him more. A handsome, worldly man and a devoted father? It made me giddy.

Within seven days of us matching online, Ty had a last-minute meeting come up at the Texas National Guard Armory near downtown Austin. His meeting was conveniently only a twenty-minute drive from my office, so we agreed on a time and place to meet. I was thrilled to meet him but at the same time a little wary, considering the method by which we'd been introduced. Everyone hears stories of online dating encounters that turn out unfavorable or even dangerous. I was excited about taking a chance and meeting him in person, but my caution was heightened. I was very nervous.

At the agreed-upon time, I parked my car and walked toward the entrance of a well-known Austin diner, a local hot spot. As I rounded the corner, there he was waiting for me. My eyes saw what I would characterize as Captain America dressed in Army fatigues. He was leaning against the wall with his hands shoved in his pockets waiting for me. When he realized it was me walking up the sidewalk, he flashed this gorgeous million-dollar smile. *Wow.* The thoughts running through my head were, *This guy can't be for real. I mean, seriously. He's too perfect in every way.* A statuesque six-foot-three Army officer, he had sandy-blond hair, even greener eyes than me, and muscle definition I could visibly see through his impeccably pressed uniform. He greeted me with a long, affection-ate hug, like we were already lovers. Then, he leaned back without letting go and gazed directly into my eyes. From this point on, I was a goner.

I wish I could give the minute-by-minute replay here of every-thing we talked about and everything I thought about during our hour-long lunch. The truth is that my nerves were on overdrive, my heart was beating out of my chest, and I could hardly breathe in his presence so literally did he "take my breath away." There's just one thing I remember like it was yesterday, and that's when, upon taking our booth in the diner, Ty very politely asked if he might remove his fatigue jacket because he was "a bit warm." I said of course, then almost fell out of my chair at the way his Army green T-shirt hugged his abs. Excuse my language, but he was built like a brick shithouse. The moment made such an impression that even today, I still sometimes picture Ty at his peak and mourn that everything had to end the way it did.

My other lingering takeaway from that meal was that Ty's ex-wife must have been crazy to let him go. Here before me was the model all-American conservative man, charming and replete with strong morals and values. Instead of rambling at length about himself, he spoke about his three boys so often and so highly—they loved to fish and throw the football together—that I marveled at his character and selflessness. I wanted our lunch to last the rest of the day, month, and year. He, finally, had to end our time together; I couldn't pull myself away from him, even with my own work responsibilities waiting for me. As Ty left to drive back to Boerne, I headed back to the office already anticipating our next contact. It arrived in the form of an intensely romantic text before I'd even parked my car:

> *Thank you again for having lunch with me! I truly enjoyed our conversation and look forward to many more. In case I didn't say this before, you're a BEAUTIFUL lady—just incredible! … If you couldn't tell, I did not want to let go or leave your presence. Sounds weird I know since we just met, but I could have looked at you all day admiring your inner beauty and getting lost looking into your green eyes …*

I was over the moon. Later that week, he sent me this poem:

> *Your presence is an intoxicating fragrance overwhelming my senses completely. / One moment with you creates a lifetime of*

*memories. / You are what I've longed for deep within my soul. / I
hand you my heart unprotected desiring eternity with you.*

(The love bombing began. I had become a target.)

Ty's Tall Tales

Our first real dinner date left me even more mesmerized. At a restaurant halfway between Boerne and Austin in San Marcos, I learned more about Ty's life, education, and military career. He'd grown up in the San Francisco Bay area and attended Louisiana State University on a football scholarship in 1987. This didn't surprise me because he was very physically fit and his three boys played football as well. He further explained how college hadn't really suited him, so he'd ended up joining the military. During his ten years in the U.S. Air Force, he'd endured seven dangerous combat deployments, including to the Middle East as part of the Gulf War. One time, he said, his unit was ambushed by two martyr women, one of them pregnant, and he'd been forced to take their lives to save his fellow airmen. It was a memory that haunted him still, every time he saw a pregnant woman in public. It was also the reason he refused to hunt for sport. More recently, in his role with the U.S. Army, he'd assisted the safe return of American soldier Bowe Bergdahl, previously being held hostage by the Taliban. This story in particular impressed me since it, though not Ty's involvement, had lately made the national news.

There were stories, too, about Ty witnessing public displays of punishment overseas—like the day a local thief was sentenced to have his hands cut off via machete. The scene sounded horrific, but as Ty put it, "After a while, you become numb to the violence." He said he wanted to intervene but couldn't—that it was "just part of the local community's law and culture." He contrasted this experience with laying to rest fallen comrades in Arlington National Cemetery, a story so poignant and patriotic that I couldn't help but hang, captivated, on every word. Having no family in the military myself, I was duly impressed by what seemed like such a powerful and exotic life, and by Ty himself, who I'd already decided was an American hero. I never questioned his stories because I didn't know enough, then, to know they didn't always make sense. I was also, if I'm honest, a wee bit intimidated by his authority.

What I did question, at times, was Ty's interest in me. His life was full of excitement and intrigue. Mine seemed boring in comparison. There I was, just a single mom working a high-tech corporate job and trying to build financial security for my retirement. How ho-hum, when my date was on active duty. But Ty didn't see it that way. For every story he shared, he begged me to share one of mine. He listened carefully, asked thoughtful follow-up questions, and complimented my abilities or my tenacity or my beauty constantly. In a word, he made me feel special. There were no warning signs that he was "selfish" or anything less than sincere.

(Narcissists are boastful with a heightened sense of self-importance. They are pathological liars, tell grandiose stories, and elaborate on top of truths. Admiration is vital to their need for

supply. They have a skewed sense of identity and can easily compartmentalize fantasy from reality.

Years later, the private investigator for my annulment case was unable to find any confirmation of Ty being awarded a football scholarship to LSU. There was no concrete military record showing combat or that Ty had taken lives during intense gun fire. As a matter of fact, there was no indication of Ty being in live combat at all. It was explained that the closest he ever got to a firing line was post-confrontation, when casualties were on-site for retrieval. This was during a three-month temporary duty (TDY) assignment. Granted, the TDY assignment was tragic and heart-wrenching. Just imagine collecting dead bodies for processing. But, Ty's stories of his military career and accomplishments were much different from his distorted reality. In actuality, Ty served in the role of security as Air Force military police and was an E5-rank sergeant in the Texas Army National Guard, not a military officer as he had claimed.

On subsequent dates, other tales (which may or may not be true, I don't know) of Ty's early taste for adventure and heroism emerged. In high school, he said, he was a volunteer firefighter in the Sierra Nevadas near Yosemite, where his family owned a mountain house. During the winter season, he worked as a weekend ski instructor at the Heavenly Resort in South Lake Tahoe. Once, he claimed, he happened upon a fatal car accident and saved a cold, crying infant—the sole survivor of the wreck—

by wrapping it in his high school letter jacket. After the first responders arrived, they took the child still wrapped in his jacket and he never saw either one again. All of Ty's tales were valiant in nature and designed to showcase his heroism.)

A Blue Sling

In between the small talk and Ty's tall tales during our first dinner date, I probed deeper into his marital history. I was less concerned about the reasons for his divorce (I'd been through one myself, after all, and understood they could be tricky) and more concerned about his intentions vis-à-vis me. I had no interest in being a rebound girl should it turn out he wasn't over his last relationship. No woman wants to waste her time being the transition person for an emotionally bruised man, regardless of how gorgeous he is. Ty assured me I was not a rebound girl, claiming his marriage was "emotionally over long ago," even though they'd only been divorced for about a year. Taking his words as truth, I couldn't wait for our next date.

(Our relationship started as a lie from the beginning. Ty was married and still living at home with his wife and their three boys. His wife had told him only a few weeks earlier that she wanted a divorce, at which point Ty had created a profile on several dating sites and begun his hunt for someone else before their divorce proceedings were even initiated. It's typical narcissistic behavior to search for new supply before the old supply has run out, and to

cut ties without looking back. Ty took no time to mourn the loss of his twenty-two-year marriage and in the blink of an eye, he found me. I was completely unaware that Ty was married during our first eight months of dating, or that I was the target for his new source of supply. He carefully placed me in his narcissistic incubator and began controlling my environment little by little.

Sometime post-annulment, I was talking to Ty's ex-wife and she apologized for not telling me Ty is a sociopath. She held back, she said, because she thought I wouldn't believe her, and she was right. Had she told me back then that he may have lied about being "attacked" in their yard in the middle of the night, going so far as to give himself a self-inflicted head injury, I would've doubled down on my assertion that she was crazy. But that's what narcissists do: They divert attention by manufacturing drama to generate sympathy. At least I can say Ty was never physically abusive, to his ex-wife or to me.)

Several weeks after our first dinner date, Ty's unit, the U.S. Army South Signal Corps, was sent to the jungles of Columbia on a mission involving a drug cartel. The mission seemed both sudden and dangerous and I was immediately concerned, especially after he told me he'd be out of communication due to the mission's "covert nature." A week after he left for Columbia, I received a call from a 1-800-number that turned out to be Ty. "I'm calling from a satellite phone in Panama," he said. Apparently there'd been an explosion while his unit was approaching the cartel compound.

He was waiting for a transport plane back to Brook Army Medical Center (BAMC) at Fort Sam Houston to have his injuries checked out.

"Injuries?" I cried, going straight to the worst.

Ty explained the explosion had thrown him against a wall. He'd lost consciousness, and had a slight concussion as well as a dislocated shoulder. *Whoa.* Welcome to life in a relationship with an active-duty military officer! His call time was limited; he had to go. I stayed in the dark about what happened next until Ty showed up on my doorstep, his left arm in a blue sling, the grin I was falling in love with on his face. My heart poured out to him as I wrapped him in a hug, my self-sacrificing American hero.

(Unbeknownst to me, the sling was Ty's first theatrical prop. He was setting the stage for using my own compassion and empathy against me. There would be many more props in the years to come, with the biggest being a wheelchair. I later learned that Ty's mission to Columbia, like all of the deployments and combat missions he claimed, were completely fabricated. His shoulder was fine. The federal special agents investigating Ty for fraud would tell me his career was, and I quote, "extremely embellished.")

Absolute Heaven

As a longtime single mom concerned for her son's and her own safety, I was always on high alert. I'd honed a sixth-sense-like awareness of potential threats and red flags. Ty never so much as made a blip on my uber-mom radar. I felt protected by him. It was a refreshing feeling to know someone was watching my back. Everywhere we went, Ty held my hand and insisted that I wait for him to open my car door before I got in. He was adamant that he walk on the outside of the sidewalk to protect me from run-away cars. Even though there are rarely run-away cars, I thought this notion was very gallant. While at my home, he always ensured that all the doors were locked and secured before we went to sleep at night. When we were out and about in restaurants or in public spaces, he could point out all the hidden surveillance cameras that typically go unnoticed by the naked eye. He even pointed out some hidden surveillance cameras that I was never able to see or locate. I thought his heightened observation skills jived with his years of military training and appreciated how seriously he took my security. I always felt safe when I was with Ty.

Our next several months together were absolute heaven. My dreams and prayers had come true. I thanked God every day for bringing a man like Ty into my life. Ty had every quality I'd ever hoped for in a man. He was loving, affectionate, romantic, attentive, handsome, giving, selfless, sexy, doting, and complimentary, plus every other "perfect man" adjective. While we never discussed it, I assumed he was financially stable considering he lived in a 4000+-square-foot-home on several acres of land with a guest house, a custom pool, and a sports court on the property and drove a loaded 4x4 Dodge Ram truck. How was I to know the house was the one he shared with his executive-level ex-wife, or that she had bankrolled his extravagant lifestyle? Sure, if I offered to pay for a meal out or one of our many weekend escapes to a Texas Hill Country bed and breakfast, he let me and never argued. I thought that meant he believed in equality, underscored by our dozens of meet-in-the-middles for an intimate dinner during our busy workweek schedules. His devotion to spending time with me was above and beyond. I appreciated his grand efforts. After all, he was juggling an Army career and three very active boys who I understood had been left emotionally devastated by their parents' divorce.

(Ty always came my direction or we met in the middle because he was still living at home with his wife and three boys. I was a secret he didn't want discovered. To make sure it stayed that way, Ty told me it wasn't allowed, by order of the military, for him to have social media or for me to post pictures of him to my own social media channels. The risk that his face, as an officer involved in top-secret military operations, would be recognized was too great. He could become a target, endangering not only his life but the lives of those around him. Clever story. It worked. Out of respect for this policy, I never posted any pictures of us together and remained the secret Ty wanted me to be.)

Ty didn't have to tell me twice about his boys' mental state. Being the empty nester of a son myself, I understood it takes time for the children of divorce to recover and emotionally rebuild. Ty expressed feeling "brokenhearted" that his sons were experiencing more distress than one might expect from a typical divorce and said frequently, "Everything I do, I do for my family." His ex-wife he defined as a "functioning alcoholic" and "neglectful mother" who had abandoned the boys to climb the corporate ladder. Ty had convinced her to try marriage counseling, and right up until the divorce proceedings began, the whole family held out hope that she'd want to be a part of their lives again. In the end, all his efforts to repair his marriage and save the family had been in vain. I felt for their collective trauma while at the same time feeling grateful Ty had at least received 50/50 custody. It meant there was less time for "us," but a boy needs his father in his life.

(Ty's sons were actually coping well. He was using his children's invented emotional state as another sympathetic ploy to keep me away from Boerne, Texas. Also, while it was true Ty had received joint custody, he wasn't liable for child support. After the annulment, I asked his ex-wife why she had allowed him to forgo child support. She said it was because she supported the boys on her own anyway and she just wanted out of that marriage quickly.)

Two Bubbles

With the ex-wife out of the picture, Ty had become his sons' primary protector. For this reason, he requested that I wait until the boys were emotionally stable before I meet them, his family, or his friends. It was important to Ty that the timing be perfect when I met the boys for the first time. He didn't want them to hear from outside sources that he was seeing someone, claiming it would only add to their distress. On the one hand, I empathized with and respected this wish. On the other, Ty had met my son, family, and friends within the first few months of our relationship, and I was eager to get to know the people he cared about as well.

(This should have been the first red flag, but I neglected to see the signs due to positive mirroring. Ty was incredibly charming and believable, thanks to blinding levels of love bombing. The story about his wife being a functioning alcoholic and neglectful mother was pure fabrication. In reality, his soon-to-be ex-wife was the primary financial provider for Ty and their three boys. She even provided housing for and supplemented the livelihood of Ty's mother. After my annulment was granted, I was told that Ty had been looking for his next meal ticket before his ex-wife had even initiated their divorce proceedings. And, he'd found me. He had secured his new supply.

Looking back, I recognize that God was speaking to me. A few strangers in a restaurant once tried to warn me that Ty was married with a casual comment they made as they were paying their bill. They leaned over next to our table and said to Ty, "Good luck with your wife." As the men walked away, Ty and I looked at each other, confused. He didn't seem to know them and thought it was a case of mistaken identity. So, we laughed it off and continued enjoying our dinner. However, they knew he was married and had vocalized it.

Another missed indicator was during a Texas Rangers baseball game in Arlington, Texas. A few months after Ty and I had met, my parents invited us to a game so they could meet Ty in a fun public setting. Our seats ended up catty-corner behind a family Ty knew from Boerne. This family (including the children) kept turning around and staring at us the entire game. They spent more time looking at us than watching the game. At the time, I thought they were just curious. But that wasn't it at all. They knew he was married and were acquaintances with his wife. The children played with his boys. I was unaware.

A year later, I'd be formally introduced to this family for the first time at one of Ty's son's baseball games. They wouldn't say anything about meeting at the Rangers game and I would have no reason to bring it up, either. Only when everything came out would I remember how restless and jittery Ty was that day, how often he got up to use the restroom or go to the concession stand. He hadn't even wanted to go to the game, citing a debilitating migraine, but I'd told him he needed to "grin and bear it" since my family had driven for hours and spent a lot of money on tickets and hotel rooms to come meet him. After the annulment, the timing of his migraine made me wonder if he knew there was a risk of seeing Boerne people at that game.)

Until I got to meet his three boys in person, Ty did a great job including me in their lives virtually. Every week, he sent photos of and other updates about their sporting events, fishing adventures, and what was happening at school. In this way, I grew to know their faces and to an extent their personalities long before I ever got to hug them. I thought they looked happy in the photos despite their evident heartbreak. And why wouldn't they? They had the world's greatest dad. Almost every time he sent one of those photos, Ty added how he hoped I would be a part of their family outings soon, that he was anxious for the day when the boys would be emotionally stable enough.

(Early in our relationship, Ty used to talk about his "two bubbles." I was one bubble and the other bubble was the boys. I never really understood this strange analogy, but as I look back on various conversations, it's almost as if he was subconsciously hinting that he was living two lives. He was a shape-shifter switching from one life to another as he drove between two cities and balanced two separate personalities—the price of preventing his two bubbles from intersecting and bursting.)

Nine o'Clock Calls

As time passed, I fell hard for Ty. Two things I loved about him were his broad intelligence and clockwork reliability. Ty was a meticulous thinker and proficient at almost everything. I felt as if his military background had given him more insight and hands-on experience than other men. We could talk for hours and it was energizing being able to have challenging conversations on a multitude of topics. On nights when we were apart, he made sure we talked on the phone at nine o'clock sharp. Nine o'clock gave him time to feed the boys, help them complete homework, and get the younger two tucked into bed. I admired that parenting was his number-one priority and appreciated how his consistency allowed me, a very structured person, to stick to routines, too. It also had its downsides, of course. Occasionally, nine would be inconvenient for me and I'd call earlier hoping to catch him, but he either wouldn't answer or would text me back saying, "I'm busy with the boys. I'll call you at nine o'clock." So, I let that ball be in his court.

(Narcissists are "know it alls" even when they don't know it all. They can speak with confidence and conviction on topics about which they know nothing. Their egos lead them to believe they are more intelligent than anyone they engage, such that they usually end up lecturing you on the subject matter. Caution: Narcissists are not as smart as they appear!

While we were dating, the nine o'clock calls were intentionally planned not to interrupt Ty's family time. He couldn't risk being caught in a compromising situation. These scheduled calls continued throughout our entire four years together on days that we were apart. They rarely lasted more than five minutes and were limited to the superficial. Only after our marriage was dissolved did I understand the element of control with the nine o'clock call.)

Sixth Sense

Ty mentioned several times and on various occasions that he was born with a sixth sense. He believed he had the ability to sense when things were about to happen, or alternatively, to sense things from a person's past. "I'm intuitive," he told me. I didn't quite understand what he meant until one evening when we were sitting on my couch talking. He said he had a very strong intuition that there was once a Labrador retriever that had lived in my house. And that at one time, my front formal dining area was configured as a TV room. He said the kitchen countertops weren't always granite and had previously had a wooden border. Outside my home, he sensed the hot tub in the backyard had not been there when I bought the house. "I feel like maybe you installed it about five years ago?" he questioned.

I remember getting very, very still when Ty said these things because there was no way he could have known any of that. None! Unless he indeed had a sixth sense. Yes, years before I'd had a beautiful yellow Lab named Gunnar. He'd since passed away. And, Ty was right … the front formal dining room had once been a TV room used by my son and his friends to play video games. Sometime after purchasing my home, I had remodeled and updated the kitchen with granite. I'd installed the hot tub and the deck in the backyard *exactly* five years prior. How could he have known any of that?

Being a person of faith, I was tempted to see his "gift" as God-given. Although I'm not overly religious, I'm deeply spiritual, and I do believe some individuals can possess special abilities, have extra-sensitive perception, or receive premonitions. While I find these people interesting, I still always listen to "sixth-sense stories" with skepticism—except for when it came to the man I was dating. Ty had told me everything with such pin-point accuracy. Who other than God could impart such knowledge? At the time, it further heightened my amazement of Ty … like he was a superhero on top of being a military hero. Now, knowing what I know, I feel so dumb for believing him.

(If my positive mirroring hadn't been full throttle, I would have realized that everything Ty said he'd "sensed" could be divined from old pictures in the upstairs closet. Ty had been at my house alone that day when I was at work. He'd simply grasped the opportunity to paw through my stuff—including a pile of home renovation photographs with date stamps.)

"Hawk"

Many evenings, Ty would drive to my house directly from the Army base in San Antonio. He would typically still be dressed in Army fatigues when he arrived. Being an officer with very busy demands on base, he rarely had time to change into civilian clothes before his drive. I never took it upon myself to ask him about all the insignia or patches on his uniform. I probably wouldn't have understood it, anyway. There were so many Army and military acronyms he threw at me in casual conversation that I would more than likely have ended up confused. But, one day when his Army fatigues were laying across the stairs, he asked me if I was interested in learning about the insignia. Ty then described in detail what each pin and patch represented. There were pins for completing various trainings and certifications and patches for all sorts of military honors. In addition to having Army Ranger and Special Forces training, my boyfriend was a paratrooper, a certified rescue diver, and a sharpshooter. He had abnormally precise vision, he said, which made him an expert marksman with perfect accuracy—a skill that had earned him the call-sign of "Hawk." Once again, I was in awe of everything Ty had accomplished. It was incredible to me that a man in his mid-40s could still possess these physical attributes.

My family was just as enamored with Ty. You could say he was "courting" them as well as me, and for his stories alone he was a favorite at every family get-together. He never tired of telling and we never tired of listening to tales of rappelling from Black Hawk helicopters, infiltrating enemy territory, gathering intelligence, and rescuing hostages. His description of SERE (Survival, Evasion, Resistance, and Escape) training made an especially strong impression as he related being forced to endure starvation, sleep deprivation, physical abuse, and other forms of torture, all so he would be "ready" were he ever taken hostage himself. While evading capture during one days-long training exercise, he told us, he ate a banana peel out of a trash can to keep his strength up. During the interrogation portion, he was beaten, resulting in a black eye and a dislocated left shoulder. (Yes, the same one he "dislocated" in Colombia; Ty often told different versions of the same stories or invented different takes on the same traumas.) The reason Ty had to go through all of this, he said, was because he was so important to the military. The amount of sensitive military intelligence he possessed put him at high risk for enemy capture. Truly, my family, friends, and I thought, Ty was a person to be admired by all. And still so humble despite everything!

Subconsciously, I felt I wasn't good enough to be with a man like Ty. Why, when he could have any woman he wanted, had he chosen me? Yet, the fact that he had thrilled me and made me proud. I was lucky—lucky to be with him, and later, lucky to be free of him.

(Post-annulment, I was informed that most of the insignia on Ty's Army fatigues were old and outdated. My legal team speculated he may have obtained them online, at a thrift store, or on the military base. He had not, at any rate, earned the badges he wore. They also don't believe he wore the pins and patches to work, as he would have stood out immediately. It's likely he added them to his uniform on the way home each day to impress me—another stage prop.

Ty's narcissistic performance was so elaborate that during our first month together, he feigned night terrors, during which he would kick frantically and moan with fear. One night he pushed me completely out of the bed. He explained these terrors were the result of being bound and caged during SERE training, as well as his multiple combat missions. However, the phenomenon was short-lived and abruptly stopped. I only experienced a few in the beginning and they never returned. Ty's reasoning was that I was the only person capable of comforting him while he slept. "Your presence gives me peace," he said, lying to me as he spooned me.)

Heartstrings and Hot Buttons

An opportunity arose when I was hosting a corporate retirement party to introduce Ty to my friends and co-workers, all of whom would be in the same place at the same time. Ty was working at Fort Sam Houston that day but promised to drive from San Antonio to Austin to join us. I couldn't wait for my co-workers and friends, who for eighteen years had known me as a single mom, to meet the man in my life, a military hero. When he walked through the venue's entryway, I was a little surprised to see him still dressed in his Army fatigues. I thought he would have had time to change before the event. "I'm sorry," he apologized in private. "I got sidetracked and got a late start." It didn't matter; he was there, that was the important bit. Excited, I introduced him around the group, then left him to chat with my longtime friend and professional mentor, another retired Army warrant officer like Ty. I thought they might have a lot in common. They did, Ty assured me. He'd had a good evening, and everyone I talked to said they'd enjoyed meeting Ty, especially the women. I was extremely proud.

(Years later, my mentor/friend told me he'd known that night there was something very odd about Ty's military patches and insignia. "He was wearing an Army Ranger tab on his left shoulder," my friend said, "as well as high-speed insignia you typically see on Special Forces soldiers"—including a combat action

badge, master parachute badge, freefall parachute badge, and a diver badge. But after talking to Ty, he didn't believe Ty had the experience or training to support those badges. Sure enough, the private investigator my attorney hired gained access to Ty's DD-214 military separation paperwork, which revealed that Ty was never in Special Forces, never attended Army Ranger school, and did not have the right to wear their insignia. Further, he was misrepresenting himself as a WO1 when the separation paperwork confirmed he was an E5 sergeant, a low-level non-commissioned officer. The legal term for this type of misrepresentation is "stolen valor," and I've since learned it's punishable as a military crime.)

During one of our weekend drives, Ty took me on the Army base at Fort Sam Houston and showed me the building where he worked. As it was a Sunday afternoon, no one else was around. We had the building to ourselves as he badged in and gave me a tour of his area, the command stations, and the briefing rooms. In each room, he educated me on all of the top-secret decisions that were made there. I asked him if I, a civilian visitor, was allowed to enter top-secret areas and he said yes since I was accompanied by a military officer. As it was, there were no security personnel in the building to hold me back, so I gladly took the tour of the U.S. Army South Signal Corps command center.

(It didn't take long for Ty to become an expert on me, Dee Ashby. But then I was an open book who hid nothing. I was vocal about my likes, dislikes, opinions, and beliefs, and made it easy for Ty

to school himself on every detail of what motivated me. Soon, he knew what pulled my heartstrings—my son, romantic gestures, Hallmark movies, human kindness, dogs, a beautiful sunset— and pushed my hot buttons—passive-aggressive and judgmental behavior, sarcasm, political discussions, animal cruelty. He became quick to play to my sympathies, all in the name of controlling and manipulating situations and conversations. Because I was oblivious to mirroring as a narcissistic tactic, I found it amazing and almost a miracle that Ty had my exact same likes and dislikes. From favorite foods and tastes in home décor to religious views and parenting styles, we agreed on everything—or so I thought. I didn't know he'd molded himself into my perfect man, that we were compatible because he was holding up a mirror.)

Ruined

Romance poured out of Ty like a cascading waterfall. A summer afternoon picnic on a blanket with wine and cheese yielded our initials being carved into a tree along the Pedernales River. This incredibly thoughtful and loving gesture took him almost an hour to complete with a small pocketknife. That autumn, when bright leaves covered the back lawn, Ty cleared a path through them to create a giant heart with an arrow piercing its center. The heart was too large to be visible from the ground, so he led me to my bedroom balcony overlooking the backyard so I could see it. There were mornings I would go downstairs to find random items—strawberries, candies, utensils, cotton balls, wine

corks—arranged in the shape of a heart on the kitchen counter, or step out of the shower to see sexy messages written in lipstick on the mirror. Once, a surprise trail of rose petals led me to a waiting bubble bath. Every time, these gestures took my breath away. I was astonished again and again by the trouble he'd take to do something so sweet. After enough of them, I knew that just like the tree that bore our initials would never be the same, my heart and soul would never return to the way they'd been before. I'd been ruined by this flawless man. And to think—our relationship was still in its infancy! We had the rest of our lives to be together.

(Our first year together consisted of rapid consumption and unadulterated entrapment courtesy of love bombing. Only two short weeks after we met, Ty told me he loved me. I didn't return the sentiment at first because I thought it was too fast, but it didn't take long before I was genuinely extending the feelings that came with the words. Within no time, he was telling me he loved me so often that it almost became annoying. It was overkill, as if he couldn't say it enough. Ty was all-consuming and saturating.)

Beyond being the absolute best at amorous gestures, Ty also showered me with compliments and kind words daily. He sent text messages or emails with love songs linked and insisted I listen to them as they "reminded him of me." He slipped secret love notes into my purse for me to find when I least expected them. One time on a flight to California's wine country, our airplane seats got separated due to overbooking and Ty had the attendant bring me a handwritten note on a napkin: "The man in 3E loves the girl in 20B," it read. The attendant was giddy over Ty's note and she wasn't even the recipient, leading the passengers around me to start applauding!

Ty's courtesy extended to the bedroom, where he would always ask before he touched me. "Can I kiss you?" he might say. "Can I hold your hand? Can I hug you?" I thought it was silly at the same time as I respected his consideration. I wished every woman could have a man like Ty in their life. If they did, I mused, the world would be a better place.

Mostly, Ty made sure I knew how beautiful he thought I was. Like a princess, I went to bed every night with my pillows fluffed and my covers turned down for me, and woke up every morning to Ty telling me I was beautiful. No woman feels beautiful in the morning, but he always made me feel like I was. I remember telling a friend how long I'd waited to find someone who "deserved" me, but I was the one who didn't deserve Ty. He was everything I'd ever prayed for, plus much more.

(Even knowing what I do now about narcissistic patterns, I still marvel at Ty's wonderful gestures. Normal trusting women never would have suspected that these gestures were not genuine but instead meant to lure and seduce for the purpose of entrapment and personal gain. Narcissists do not put forth effort unless it will benefit them in the near or long term. In my case, what Ty wanted and stood to gain from me was everything. All my time, all my emotions, my growing 401(k), and the farm and ranch

land I would one day inherit from my parents. Even before we were married, he truly believed that everything I had belonged to him. My mistake was letting him make me think it belonged to him, too. Ty was smart, strategic, clever, and cunning. A master manipulator. A classic narcissist. The ultimate conman and predator. I was the perfect prey he molded like potter's clay.)

Most evenings when we were together, we would fill to-go cups with wine and take a "wine walk" as the sun was setting. These wine walks gave us undistracted moments to talk about our next steps and make future plans for all four of our boys. Often during these walks Ty would say things like, "We're soulmates," "You're the only one who understands me," and "You saved me at just the right time." I agreed we were soulmates born to find each other, but I hadn't saved Ty. If anything, I thought, he had saved me.

(Narcissists use elaborate gestures and gift-giving as "investment tactics" to win over their victims or distract them from what's really happening behind the scenes. It keeps the victim off-guard so their natural instinct of caution doesn't kick in, allowing the narcissist to maintain positive emotional control. Eventually, they have enough "trust equity" built that the victim will be completely loyal. Ty was VERY, VERY good at this! It was his prize tool in his toolbox. His romantic gestures continued throughout our four years together and up until the day I abruptly left.)

2

JETWAY TO GERMANY

"Beware of perpetrators in disguise. ... Some people set fires wherever they go, and have mastered the art of playing the burn victim." —Steve Maraboli

The day finally came when Ty was ready to introduce me to the boys. Having heard about them for almost a year and having seen dozens of their pictures, I was so excited I could hardly contain myself. I felt as if I already knew them. Ty introduced me to his oldest son first. We met at a Hill Country hamburger joint outside of Fredericksburg, Texas that had become a favorite meet-in-the-middle spot for Ty and me. The following week, Ty brought all three boys to Austin so I could show them the local hot spots around downtown. As it was the end of November, the weather was mild and beautiful. When they all arrived, I couldn't wait for them to ring the doorbell, so I walked outside to greet them as they were getting out of the truck. All three boys plus Ty handed me a single long-stemmed red rose. Even though I knew Ty was the instigator, the gesture melted my heart. The boys' personalities perfectly matched their pictures. They were funny, smart, and full of energy; everything Ty had described. As our day together unfolded, I understood why Ty was so proud and protective. The boys were indeed the light of his life. They loved Ty with the same intensity that he had for them.

(Unbeknownst to me, I met the boys exactly two weeks after Ty's divorce had been finalized in mid-November. I don't know what he'd told them about me or how long the boys thought we'd been dating, but I know I was still a secret he kept from most everyone else. The first several occasions I got to spend time with the boys, we always met in the middle or in Austin; I was not yet allowed to participate in their lives in Boerne, Texas. Ty had introduced me to his mother several months earlier, but again, we'd met at a restaurant outside the city limits.

I'd taken an instant liking to his mother, by the way. She was sweet, loving, and a tight hugger. It didn't surprise me that she was so inviting because these were attributes I recognized in Ty. His mother said she was happy to meet me and glad that Ty had met someone like me "after all he'd been through with his ex-

wife." That she reinforced her son's story about Ty being the victim of his ex-wife made me feel even more sympathetic toward Ty as well as needed and wanted by him—and his mother!)

Laid Off

Like a speeding train barreling down its track, the love Ty and I had for each other grew stronger and more unstoppable each day. We would depend on that love to see us through one distressing event after another as, outside of our relationship, Ty's personal life began to fall apart. First, the Army announced they were eliminating positions at Fort Sam Houston due to budget cuts and Ty's job was one of them. It seemed unusual that the military would lay off an enlisted officer, but I didn't know anything about government budgets so I assumed it was like the corporate world: When budgets decrease, so does the workforce. Then, in the middle of scrambling to find a new job, the home Ty had previously shared with his ex-wife went under contract to be sold. It was December and he had to rush to find another residence for the boys before the Christmas holidays. My heart broke for him. He'd lost his job and now the family home, and he was dealing with everything alone. I would have liked to help him, but Ty stressed that I already was. "Your love," he said, "is all that's saving me from despair." To his other bubble, his boys, he said, "I am the tower; everything goes through me." It's how he maintained balance, control, and a single line of communication—while keeping me far away from the scene in Boerne.

Thank goodness, Ty found a rental home and was able to move before the holidays arrived. I strongly insisted on helping him move, but he even more sternly pushed back and told me it was something he needed to do on his own for the purposes of closure. Although the transition to the rental home was difficult for Ty and the boys, who were used to much grander accommodations, after they got settled was when the door finally opened and I was able to visit Boerne, Texas. This was when I began integrating into the lives of the boys and was invited into their dynamic.

(I learned post-annulment that Ty's ex-wife paid the monthly lease for Ty's rental home during this time. She was still providing him with financial support even after their divorce for the benefit of the boys. As for the "layoff," what I learned after the annulment was that until this point, Ty had been an "active" National Guard Reservist working in the Signal Core for SOUTHCOM. The Army can activate a Reservist to full-time Army just like they can remove a Reservist from full-time Army and place them back on "reserve." This is what happened with Ty: He'd been activated to full-time Army and then deactivated, which was when he'd filed for unemployment.)

One Step Forward, Two Steps Back

At least Ty had a place to call home again, but even that relief was short-lived. Within weeks of moving in, his expensive top-of-the-line Dodge Ram 4x4 truck was stolen. His oldest son had been driving the truck for the weekend (as he was accustomed to doing when out with friends, on a date, or needing to haul things) when it was discovered missing from the parking lot where he was staying. On top of this upset, Ty's insurance company was in dispute with the police report and wouldn't provide him with a rental car, leaving him without reliable transportation. He was able to use his oldest son's small car sometimes, but when his son needed the car, I let Ty share my vehicle. I worked remotely from home most days and didn't need it during the day. It was the least I could do for Ty, whose bad luck kept getting worse.

(This is when Ty first began to use me for my resources and advertise himself as a victim of circumstance. The Army was to blame for his lost job, his ex-wife was to blame for his failed marriage and lost home, an auto thief was to blame for his stolen truck, and the insurance company was to blame for not providing a rental car. Blinded by his love-bombing, I felt so bad for Ty I didn't see the reality for what it was. Ty's truck had NOT been stolen. Years later it was confirmed the truck had been repossessed by the bank after an entire year of nonpayment. There was no auto insurance dispute. He'd lied and elaborated on top of his lie to play the victim. He never admitted the truth.)

Another Blow!

Another blow! The black cloud hovering over Ty would not go away. The Texas Army National Guard out of Bee Cave, Texas

57

announced they were reactivating him (yay!) but deploying him to Stuttgart, Germany for a dangerous six-month mission with Special Operations Detachment-Africa (boo!). This deployment had potential to extend for a year. He would be based at U.S. Army Garrison Stuttgart and rotate with his team in and out of Afghanistan. His mission was to train the Afghan Army on how to use signal and communications equipment. With just one short month to prepare to leave for Germany, Ty was forced into another transition, rushing to move out of the rental house he had just moved into, put everything he owned in storage, and get the boys settled with their mother 100% before his departure. Ty's life was starting to morph from that of Captain America into Captain Chaos. The never-ending drama was like a game of Whack-a-Mole. He couldn't whack the mallet fast enough to keep all the moles down.

(After Ty's forced exit from his role at Fort Sam Houston, he began drawing unemployment benefits from the Texas Workforce Commission. Then, he sought out and was able to get a "paid assignment" with the National Guard out of Bee Caves, Texas. Ty sold this activity to friends and family as a "dangerous deployment" that he had no choice in, when in fact he'd not only applied for the TDY like any civilian applying for a job on indeed.com, but he would never leave the relative comfort of a German hotel.)

Ty's closest friends and some acquaintances in Boerne gathered to give him a surprise going-away party. I felt honored to be asked by the host and hostess to help participate in the surprise.

At this point, my relationship with Ty was over a year old and the two hosts were the only friends of Ty's I had met. They were a lovely Christian couple and they both embraced me as a newcomer with open arms. They even encouraged me to invite my family and friends into their home to honor Ty's departure. I thought this was very courteous since they barely knew me. I was able to help orchestrate getting Ty to the deployment party without him knowing. When we arrived, Ty was very surprised and touched to see about thirty people in attendance in his honor. It felt good to finally meet Ty's social network for the first time. And, they seemed curious, inquisitive, and happy to meet me as well.

All but the first few months of our relationship had been a whirlwind as Ty's string of unfortunate personal and military events continued. Now, the man I loved was being deployed to Europe and then on to the Middle East. This was an unexpected turn, but I was ready to fully support him. I even put a yellow ribbon around the oak tree in my front yard. I was very proud of him, but scared for him at the same time as he was going into a potential danger zone.

The dreaded day came in early June when he was scheduled for departure. Ty had already said his goodbyes to the boys, family, and friends, so we were able to have a quiet moment together as he prepared to leave. It was a surreal feeling driving Ty to the Austin airport for his flight to Germany. Knowing it would be six months to possibly a year before I would see him again, I was dazed. For his part, Ty seemed indifferent and emotionless, as if he was just going away for the weekend. He kept conversation light and jovial and held my hand during the entire drive to comfort me. Luckily, the airline let me go past security and sit in the terminal with him until he boarded his flight. The airlines make this exception for the family members of military personnel departing on assignments as long as they have the proper paperwork. I was grateful for that unexpected extra time with Ty before he walked down the jetway to Germany.

(It was discovered that Ty was not considered "deployed" in the terms most understand as leaving for a combat operation in a war zone. He was on a temporary duty assignment with the Texas Army National Guard—the civilian equivalent of extended travel for a business trip, training, or a conference. While on TDY, Ty was housed among civilians at the Dormero Hotel near a popular retail sector in Stuttgart, Germany that also served as corporate housing for business travelers. Ty did not live on any military base or installation while in Germany.)

While Ty was deployed in Germany, the boys' mother gave me permission to take them to the Texas panhandle for a long July 4th weekend celebration at Lake Tanglewood. It was great having all four of our boys (my college-age son and Ty's three boys) together at the same time. They'd met briefly in Austin once when my son was home from college, but this was a chance for them to really get to know each other. They got along famously, seeming to genuinely enjoy each other's company, which was comforting for me to see. We spent time on the lake, enjoyed some BBQ, watched a parade and the fireworks, and met up with my life-long friend Sandy. My hope was that this trip would take our minds off of Ty being at risk on the other side of the world. While enjoying our holiday at Lake Tanglewood, however, I received a phone call from Ty. He would be heading into Afghanistan within twenty-four hours, he said, and didn't know when he would next be able to contact us. All four boys were immediately worried, so I was glad we were surrounded by friends. The holiday happenings kept us focused on (or distracted by, depending on how you look at it) the July 4th events. Although the trip to the Texas panhandle was wonderful and everyone enjoyed it, we remained unnerved by Ty's news. It was a bittersweet trip that brought me and all four boys closer while Ty went further away.

(Military records, Ty's bank transactions, and his online social media activity all confirmed that Ty never went to Afghanistan while he was on TDY in Germany. He created an event for the sake of drama and to make sure he remained the center of attention while I, the boys, and a group of friends celebrated. Even from far away he was exercising his narcissistic skill for emotional control. He lied to all of us that day and he continued the lie throughout our marriage.)

A Very Slight Limp

Ty returned to Germany from Afghanistan without incident, but thereafter, my biggest fear came true. He was admitted to the emergency room at the civilian hospital in Stuttgart with a severe headache, a head contusion, and weakness—apparent side effects of the "extreme heat" and "physical exertion" that Ty said he and his unit had endured while in Afghanistan. He explained he had just gotten back to his hotel room when he started fading in and out of consciousness, and the next time he regained consciousness, he called his Joint Operations Center (JOC) and the hotel front desk to ask for help. The hotel personnel on duty called the ambulance. When the medics arrived, they found him blacked out and completely unconscious. Because many of his symptoms mimicked a stroke, that was the first thing his doctors ruled out at the hospital. Ty had not suffered a stroke, they said, nor could they find any root cause for any of his symptoms. They discharged him once all of his ailments had disappeared.

Ty and I were able to Skype after he was discharged from the ER and back in his hotel room. When I asked him what had happened, all he was able say due to the confidential nature of his deployment was, "Have you seen the news?" Well, I had not seen the news, but soon learned there'd been an explosion at the Kabul airport that had killed seventy-two people during the same timeframe Ty had been in Afghanistan (July 2014).

Hearing this, I grew extremely worried and wanted to get on the next flight out of Austin so I could be with Ty in Germany. I didn't see the harm in traveling to visit him because after all, he was living in a hotel and not on the Army base. He'd been taken to a civilian ER and not a military medical facility. Even if he wound up back in the ER, I didn't need special military credentials to visit him at a civilian hospital. But, Ty strongly discouraged me from doing this, citing it was against military protocol.

A few days later, he had a follow-up appointment at the Army Medical Center in Landstuhl. Just like the civilian doctors, the military physicians found no evidence that Ty had suffered a stroke. Nevertheless, only two short months into his Germany assignment, Ty requested to return stateside, stating he felt he could not physically perform assigned tasks. The commander for the Texas Army National Guard approved his request and Ty returned to the U.S. prior to the completion of his mission. He arrived on a commercial flight into Austin where I was anxious to pick him up. I was relieved to see him standing tall with a big smile coming down the escalator at the airport. Ty could not get to me fast enough. As he stepped off the escalator, I noticed he had a very slight limp on his left side that was barely noticeable, almost as if he had a pebble lodged in his shoe. We loaded his belongings in the car and then drove straight to our favorite Mexican food restaurant. As Ty had been unable to get Mexican food in Germany, he had an appetite and strong craving for Tex-Mex. Over salty corn chips and garlicky salsa, I told Ty I was "more than elated" he was back. We could now continue where we had left off and start building our life together just like we had planned.

(Was this episode the first step in Ty laying the groundwork for federal disability fraud and early military medical retirement? He led us all to believe that his medical issue stemmed from dangerous and grueling physical activity at the Kabul airport while

in Afghanistan. However, military records show he was never in Afghanistan. It also doesn't seem like a coincidence that he left for Germany as school let out for the summer and returned in time for the start of football practice. Football season was a family priority. How much, if not all, of Ty's drama was self-induced and perfectly timed?

After our marriage had been dissolved, I heard yet another version of events, this one shared with one of Ty's friends. The story Ty told this woman was even more elaborate and embellished than the first. Ty claimed he had been in live combat when a hand grenade set off a massive explosion, killing a fellow soldier and injuring Ty. Ty then said he'd woken up in a military hospital where he had received a blood transfusion and undergone surgery to remove a bone fragment from his arm. The bone fragment was purportedly from the fellow soldier who had blown up right next to Ty. The surgery, he said, pointing to an old scar on his arm, had left a visible mark. When Ty's friend asked how long he was in the hospital, Ty said the military hospital had flown him stateside to Brook Army Medical Center (BAMC) in San Antonio, and that he'd been under their care "for some time." In reality, Ty flew into the Austin airport healthy as a horse. I picked him up and we went to eat Mexican food at Chuy's.)

3

WEDDING BELLS

"The things we think are certain can be illusions." —Unknown

Ty and I were married two years to the very day we met in person at the Austin diner. Having been married previously, I didn't want or need the pomp and circumstance of a wedding ceremony but Ty thought it would be good for the boys' emotional recovery to be primary participants in the union of two families. I agreed and started planning a small outdoor wedding in the Texas Hill Country. We decided on a shabby-chic outdoor venue that was in between our two cities for the convenience of family and friends from both sides.

Wedding-ring shopping was a fun experience for us. Since it

was a costly investment for two symbols that we would wear for the rest of our lives, we went all-out and picked beautiful rings. Mine was three carats with a cushion-cut center stone of 2.2 carats. It was stunning and putting it on made me feel like royalty. With Ty's finances in limbo since his return from Germany, I paid cash for both our rings and had them immediately insured on my home-owner's insurance policy. The jeweler sized, cleaned, and appraised our rings and we were able to pick them up the following week. With a six-month countdown before our wedding date, I was excited to wear my three-carat engagement ring for everyone to see. Ty expressed his desire to wear his ring, too. *Hmm.* I thought his request was outside of tradition, but he explained he was ready to outwardly show his commitment to me even if we weren't married yet. I thought it was a sweet sentiment, even if a bit strange. So, he put his ring on too, just like a "man's engagement ring." Six months to go!

During the time I spent planning and paying for our wedding, Ty was still unemployed. Since his return from Germany, the Army had been experiencing a process glitch and his active-duty status had been caught between two cost centers. They owed him salary and backpay that was being held in some void. Ty was also owed incapacitation pay (INCAP) for coming back from Germany with medical complications. Not wanting to add to Ty's already-heavy financial burden, I proceeded to pay for our honeymoon by dipping into my accounts. I didn't think much about dropping a large chunk of change for the combined wedding costs because I knew Ty would help me recoup the expense from the significant amount of backpay coming his way. It was just a matter of time before his salary would be freed from the Army's red-tape process.

(This was the beginning of my financial demise. It was discovered pre-annulment that while I was paying for our rings, planning our wedding, and putting a deposit down on our honeymoon, Ty was living off of credit cards. He had multiple accounts in default, as well as several accounts already in collection. It was also at this time that I traced multiple bank transactions to a full-service erotic massage parlor located in a low-income area near the San Antonio airport. During the wedding planning phase, however, and for two years after our wedding, I was unaware of any of this.)

We celebrated our wedding day on a beautiful Sunday afternoon. The Texas Hill Country landscape was solid with April bluebonnets and other wildflowers. It was the picture-perfect setting for our outdoor spring wedding. There was a hint of potential thunderstorms that worried me—we could hear the roar of thunder in the distance—but fortunately, they bypassed our outdoor venue. Many of our friends and family arrived several hours early to help set up and decorate for the ceremony and dinner reception. We hoped the wedding would not just be about us, but also bring our family and friends together, especially all four of our boys.

Ty took charge of setting up the ceremony and the altar area. At my request, he had constructed a rugged cross out of old barn wood from my dad's ranch in the Texas panhandle. Ty and my dad

had spent an entire weekend searching for the perfect wood. Then Ty had built a platform so it would stand steady at the altar. As he maneuvered it into place that day, I thought it was absolutely beautiful and full of sentiment. Not only was it handmade by Ty, but it was a powerful symbol of our faith in God. Although Ty was not really the church-going type (he'd gone a few times with me early on in our relationship, but I could tell he was out of his element and uncomfortable), he came from a faith-filled family himself and was no stranger to God or the Bible. He was therefore happy to support me at family church functions and to include God in the most important day of our lives. Our wedding vows referenced Scripture as did the centerpieces on every reception table: Bible verses I had chosen and framed. It was important to me, so it was important to Ty, that God and our faith be the center of our marriage as we brought our four boys and two families together.

As Ty and I walked down the grassy path lined with wildflowers as husband and wife for the first time, I felt my dreams had all come true. It was a day of pure happiness. That day I married the perfect man and together we had four amazing boys with distinctly different personalities. We felt very lucky that all of them were smart, healthy, and overall good kids. Now, we were a family unit. I couldn't stop smiling and kissing my new husband. Our marriage and life together had begun.

(Months before we were married, Ty had already begun perpetrating government fraud. Without my knowledge, he'd convinced his doctors during a military medical examination that

he was 100% disabled by faking symptoms he did not have. To qualify for 100% disability, one has to be unable to perform basic daily tasks like shopping, driving, or traveling without assistance, be unable to lift or carry more than twenty pounds, and be unable to sit, stand, or walk for more than two hours at a time. Ty could do all of this, of course, but he claimed he couldn't walk without the use of an assistive device, earning him Supplemental Security Income (SSI) benefits from the Social Security Administration (SSA)—fraudulent income. I didn't know about the exam or its results, and I didn't know about the income.

Once I became aware, I couldn't help but wonder ... on the day we said "I do," was Ty already planning the ideal time to become "fully handicapped" in order to physically match the verbiage on the disability claim he had already filed with the SSA? (And to be more convincing for the early military medical retirement process?) Did he want to be married before the onset of paralysis to have a solid financial safety net? Ty became full left-side paralyzed five months after our wedding. During his initial fraud interview with federal special agents from both the SSA and Veterans Administration (VA), he told them he didn't remember walking down the aisle at our wedding. His statement was unbelievable and personally crushing. There were 80+ people in attendance at our wedding who would attest that Ty was fully aware and functional that day.)

Our honeymoon to the majestic scenery of Santa Fe, New

Mexico was more like much-needed time away to rest and recoup than anything romantic. Ty and I were both exhausted from all the wedding activities, but not too tired to notice how beautiful Santa Fe is in the spring. We enjoyed the local shops, the gourmet cuisine, and the mountainous backdrop all around us. Just outside of Albuquerque, New Mexico on one sunny afternoon, we stopped at an Indian casino for a quick spin on a few slot machines, then went hiking up to the peak of the Petroglyph National Monument. I decided to treat us and splurge on a full day at Ten Thousand Waves, an exclusive luxury day spa in the foothills outside of Santa Fe. It was a pricey day that cost roughly $1,500, but my newlywed mind justified the expense. After all, it was our honeymoon!

(Ty's bank statements revealed that the day after we returned from our honeymoon, he patronized the full-service erotic massage parlor in San Antonio, Texas. The pattern was always the same. He would buy a tank of gas, pull hundreds of dollars from an ATM, then purchase a small-sum service from the parlor. That's how those establishments conduct business—they record a small transaction on their books, but the real money flows behind closed doors. Discovering this transaction years later during the annulment process literally brought me to my knees. My former husband never had any intention of honoring our vows. One week after our wedding he was already being unfaithful. That's when I knew I was a long-term con for Ty. Did he ever really love me, or did he only love what I could provide for him and his boys?)

My Credit Alone

Since Ty's return from Germany, we'd lived at my Austin home while Ty's belongings were still in storage. On the weeks when he had custody of the boys, they all stayed at Ty's mother's house in Boerne while I continued to work in Austin. The boys seemed to be okay with this temporary arrangement because they enjoyed spending time with their grandmother. As I understood it, she was more like a mother figure to them because she had taken care of them since they were infants. For the purposes of creating a more normal family environment and so the boys could have their own rooms again, Ty and I looked for an apartment in Boerne that he could use on the weeks he had custody. Luckily, we were able to find a nice complex close to the boys' school, and we started the application process. Even though the boys loved being with their grandmother, it was time for them to move out of her house and into a residence they could call their own.

A few days later, the apartment manager called to notify us that our application had been accepted on my credit alone. We were cleared to move in on the date we had chosen. Ty assured me he would be responsible for the apartment and living expenses in Boerne since he was the boys' father. It should have been easily affordable given the $2,000 he received each month in Wounded Warrior funds, plus the incapacitation (INCAP) pay and the Army backpay that were still forthcoming. I nevertheless paid the deposit and began shopping to furnish the apartment for the boys, wanting to contribute something to their happiness. I also kept full financial responsibility for my Austin home. Ty and I continued to maintain separate accounts after we were married. As long as the bills were getting paid, we agreed, there was no reason for us to commingle accounts.

(At the time, I didn't think anything about how the apartment manager had phrased her comment—"approved on your credit alone." It was a red flag and one of many blaring clues that I missed over the years. What I didn't know was that Ty's credit score was in the low 500s, a number considered poor and high-risk. The annulment process revealed that he had stopped paying on every account the month we got married, sending more accounts to collection, and yet had somehow obtained new lines of credit without making one single payment. His debt was massive and growing (and included ever more transactions made at his favorite erotic massage parlor). I never found out about the debt because Ty was hiding the collections notices that came in the mail.)

Our New Normal

On weeks when Ty had the boys, I stayed at the Boerne apartment, too. It was cumbersome commuting back and forth for work (I could work remotely except for specific days of the week, when we had strategic meetings), but it was important to me to be a part of Ty's and the boys' lives in Boerne. Even though we were using it less, I never considered selling my home in Austin. It had accumulated a lot of equity over the eighteen years I had owned it. Also, it was my son's childhood home. He and I both had an emotional attachment to the house. Ty and I therefore agreed I would commute back and forth on Tuesday and Wednesday for my work obligations. Other than those two nights each week, we would be together as a family in the Boerne apartment. This was the start of establishing our home with the boys in their community. My town-to-town commute and routine became a steady part of our lives.

(Over the duration of our five-year relationship and marriage, I drove 480+ round trips from Austin to Boerne and back, totaling more than 110,400 miles. I spent an additional 2,000+ hours in the car taking my husband to his medical appointments, visiting him in the hospital, and taking care of my stepsons. This extensive traveling took its toll on me mentally and physically while I did my best to maintain a full-time corporate job and manage two households.)

Months after our move into the Boerne apartment, summer ended and the boys went back to school. They were busy with all the sporting activities that come along with the beginning of a new school year. We had settled into our routine as a family and it felt like Ty's situation had finally leveled out, too. There was much less drama and his "black cloud" was starting to dissipate.

Unfortunately, this feeling didn't last very long. The still-pending INCAP was ultimately not approved, and the Army backpay

Ty had told me he was owed never came to fruition. Six months after it had begun, the monthly Wounded Warrior funding ceased (there had always been a cap on the total payout, I just didn't know it), and the other one-time grants Ty had received from affiliate military organizations had all been consumed. Without these sources of income, Ty wasn't able to pay the apartment rent. Because he was still considered "active duty" by the Army, however, he wasn't allowed to get a civilian job (or at least that's what Ty told me). I was absolutely floored that any military branch would tell a soldier they weren't allowed to get a job to support their family, especially when the military wasn't paying them! The whole story threw me for a loop. From what I was hearing and observing, the Army was basically forcing Ty into poverty by tying his hands behind his back.

Almost overnight, then, I became the only constant source of income for two households, two adults, and four boys. The financial uneasiness was overwhelming and I was furious with the circumstances. My suggestion was to hire an attorney to expedite the Army's process and relieve the financial hardship they were forcing upon us by not paying Ty the salary he had earned. But Ty wanted to let the process run its course, calling it "typical government bureaucracy." In his words: "I have to fight for everything I get." I found his response lackadaisical and completely unhelpful when it came to the looming financial defaults I saw on the horizon. The only other solution I could think of was for me to get a second job. As I was already making a healthy six-figure salary, working 50+ hours a week, and commuting back and forth between two cities, though, this option seemed impossible.

Finally, my frustration led to our first major blowout argument, during which I insisted Ty get a job even if it wasn't allowed, sell his oldest son's recently acquired and expensive 4X4 Ford truck that we were paying for, and dissolve two large storage units full of stuff from his previous marriage that he never used. As usual, instead of acquiescing or trying to brainstorm additional ideas, Ty attempted to smooth over and lessen the magnitude of the pending defaults, as if he could disguise the inevitable. I got so angry that I stormed out. The reality was the Boerne bills were coming due, he didn't have the funds to pay them, and he didn't seem too concerned about it. He didn't even call or text when I left that evening and drove to Austin, where I stayed a few days until I calmed down. I think Ty knew I would fold and make the payments for him. My excellent credit score (in the 800s) was also at risk, and I took too much pride in my financial stability to let it crumble. After the tension subsided, I paid the apartment rent while Ty continued to work with the Incapacitation Board and the Army to get the money they owed him.

Financial Bombshells

Tax season rolled around and come Spring 2016, it was time to file our first joint tax return as a married couple. I always get a healthy return with my voluntary withholding and deductions. We needed the bump in funds, so I was anxious to get the tax return filed earlier than normal. The analysis was done, the documents were complete, and the taxes were filed. What a huge relief! We would be getting close to $10,000 back, just as I had expected. But when the IRS deposit hit the bank account several weeks later, I was very confused because it was only one-fourth of the expected amount. *Hmm.* Perhaps there would be another deposit to follow? Maybe that payment was only a portion of what we were owed. Yet, in all my years of filing tax returns, I'd never received two separate IRS deposits. So I picked up the phone and called the IRS for clarification. After waiting hours in the queue for a representative, I got my answer. Ty had outstanding IRS debt from prior years, I learned. He also owed the Social Security Administration for SSI taxes, the Texas Workforce Commission for unemployment taxes, and his Military Star AAFES credit card had defaulted and gone to collection. There were four separate government entities that Ty owed, and they all wanted their money. Therefore, they'd taken it out of our first joint federal tax return. It was another financial surprise. My blood pressure went through the roof. What the hell was going on with Ty's financial non-disclosures?!

That night, we had another fire-hot argument that excruciatingly lasted for hours. I made Ty get on the phone with the IRS and request a document stating we'd paid in full and that he had no other IRS or government debt lurking in the shadows. Although he was put out by this request, he did it. Net-net and in summary, the tax return didn't bump up the bank account as planned and I ended up supplementing Ty's accumulated debt with my withholding and deductions. Because he was my husband, I sucked up my anger, accepted this blow, and we moved on.

(Ty's pending incapacitation and Army backpay never materialized during our entire marriage. The Army denied all of Ty's claims. When the VA later approved his 100% disability retirement with retroactive funds, Ty did share $15,000 to help cover a portion of my disbursements. However, the tax return "surprise" amounted to only a small portion of his total expenditures and was but a precursor to the larger financial bombshells to come.)

The school year for the boys was going strong and it was time for everyone to get organized for Ty's niece's wedding. Ty had the honor and privilege of walking his beautiful niece, for whom he had been a father figure her entire life, down the aisle. We were all very excited for this young woman and her future husband. They were a sweet couple with a lot of love for each other and deserved many years of happiness. The day Ty gave his niece away in marriage was a great day for Ty, the bride, and the entire family.

Two weeks after Ty lovingly walked his niece down the aisle arm in arm, it happened. Lightning had struck and our lives would never be the same. Left-side paralysis!

4

....

DO YOU SMELL PANCAKES?

"Suffering isn't an obstacle to being used by God. It is an opportunity to be used like never before." —Levi Lusko

ate in the day on an October afternoon as I was working at the corporate office in Austin, I received a call from Ty's mother. She had driven him to the emergency room at Brook Army Medical Center (BAMC) on the base at Fort Sam Houston in San Antonio. Ty was unable to move the entire left side of his body, she said, and had no sensation or feeling. His left side was completely paralyzed. The BAMC medical team was about to begin a series of tests to find out what was causing the paralysis. Sitting in my office as I listened to what was happening to my husband, I grew frantic.

Two hours on jam-packed I-35 stood between us, but after hearing this news, I couldn't get to Ty fast enough. I shot out of work like a cannonball. During my panicked drive to San Antonio, the silence was brutal not hearing from Ty or his mother. I didn't know what was happening to my husband, making for a torturous drive.

When I arrived, Ty's mother had to escort me onto the base at Fort Sam Houston. She had a military ID on his behalf; I did not. Before I walked into Ty's hospital room, she described the events leading up to the ER. Ty had taken the boys to school that morning, returned to the apartment, and made himself a cup of coffee. He had just sat down on the couch to watch the morning news when he felt a tingly sensation, like he was going to pass out. The next thing he knew, it was early afternoon. He had blacked out for what he thought must have been four or five hours. When he regained consciousness, he had a severe headache and couldn't feel his left side. I was surprised to hear that instead of calling 911, me (his wife), or his nearby mother for help, Ty had decided to make his way down three flights of stairs at the Boerne apartment with only the use of his right leg and right arm. He'd driven his car to his mother's house, where he asked her to take him to the emergency room. The Boerne ER was only ten minutes away, but Ty wanted to go to the BAMC military hospital on base—an hour's drive. Considering the magnitude of the emergency, I would have made a different decision for immediate stabilization and triage. If only I had been there when tragedy struck my husband!

As it was, no one called me, the wife of the heretofore healthy man who had suddenly become paralyzed, until after Ty was placed in a room at the BAMC ER. If either he or his mother had called me en route to the hospital, I could have made it to San Antonio two hours earlier. When I questioned why no one had reached out to me, Ty's mom said simply, "Honey, we didn't want to worry you or interrupt your workday." Her response disheartened me. On top of being worried about Ty, I felt dismissed, like I was not an invited participant in a major medical crisis involving my new husband.

(During the federal investigation, due to this and other incidents, the agents assigned to the case were highly suspicious that Ty's mother was in on his ploy—but they could never prove it.)

Guardian and Protector

When I finally got to see Ty, he was laying in bed resting with many wires and sensors adhered to his body, including an IV drip for his headache. I felt nervous until he looked up and gave me his million-dollar smile. It soothed my soul to learn that he wasn't in any pain. He said the paralysis felt like he'd received a shot of Novocain. His left hand couldn't grip anything—he was unable to move any of his fingers or toes—but there was some slight movement in the palm of his hand. Otherwise, his left side was unresponsive to all stimuli. My anxiety was running high because his symptoms mirrored my dad's when he had suffered a minor stroke a few years prior. As I had my dad's doctors, I must've asked the medical staff at BAMC dozens of questions. I'm a glutton for information and never satisfied with ambiguity or half-answers.

My motto has always been *If you don't know, find out. No excuses.*

Nothing against the BAMC nursing staff and physicians—they were amazing, and I truly believe BAMC is a world-class military medical facility full of genuinely caring people—but they didn't seem to know much more than I did. Shortly after I arrived, the nurse on duty came in to administer Ty's Lipitor. Knowing Ty didn't have any history of high blood pressure, this confused me. "How high is his blood pressure?" I asked. She looked at Ty's chart and didn't see that his pressure was out of range. But since Ty's room was located on what they considered their "heart floor," Lipitor had automatically been prescribed. "Can you please go validate that order?" I asked. Even though I'm all for Western medicine, I didn't want Ty taking any unnecessary pharmaceuticals. "It's okay," Ty said. "I'll just take whatever they give me." But my gut told me something was off. When the nurse came back, she apologized. Ty didn't need Lipitor after all. At this point, I completely took over. Our roles had reversed. My husband was paralyzed and I had assumed the role of guardian and protector.

(How in the world Ty managed to cheat the tests designed to assess his reflexes, I'll never know. His neurologist never found anything wrong with him, but with "left-side weakness" as a symptom on his discharge paperwork, there was no going back. According to the federal agents, it's rare for medical professionals to change a previous diagnosis—even if they believe they made a mistake!—because it makes them look bad and opens them up to a malpractice lawsuit.)

A Software Problem

Ty's neurologist and the rest of his medical team searched tirelessly for the root cause of Ty's paralysis. MRIs, CT scans, X-rays, and several other tests yielded nothing. There was no stroke. There were no anomalies on Ty's brain scans or indications of anything physically or chemically abnormal. While to a degree this was reassuring, we desperately wanted answers. The not-knowing was absolute torture. Two days after he'd been admitted, Neurology confirmed Ty didn't have a hardware problem, but said he could potentially have a software problem (in which synapses or electrical impulses in the brain no longer connect). This is an extremely rare condition and there was no way to verify it since the brain's electrical activity is so complex. Thus, we still had no answers.

By day four, Ty was exhausted from all of the testing and frequent vital checks and I was crawling out of my skin waiting for the doctors to determine what was wrong with him. That's when we were told Ty was being discharged. WHAT?! "Let me get this straight," I said. "My husband is completely paralyzed on his left side, he can't walk, use his left arm, or grip with his left hand, and you want to discharge him to go home?" I was livid, but mostly because I was afraid. What were we going to do? "We can't do anything else for Ty," the hospital staff explained. "He'll need continuing care and therapy. That's not what we do here."

The nurse on duty brought the discharge paperwork for Ty to sign. As I reviewed the paperwork, I saw that Ty had been admitted for an acute headache and constipation. More confusion!

Couldn't they see he was paralyzed on the left side? I told the nurse Ty would not be signing the discharge paperwork because it was inaccurate. There was no mention of left-side paralysis anywhere on the document. It was late afternoon before the documents were modified. The new wording read "acute headache, left-side weakness, and constipation." They'd used the word "weakness" instead of paralysis, but at least it was noted. I was mollified enough to allow Ty to sign and he was discharged.

(Ty's alter ego had emerged. My athletic G.I. Joe was now a disabled veteran. The sympathy he stood to garner in this new role would be his most powerful narcissistic tool yet. Ty used me and everyone who knew him as unknowing participants in building his pretend disabled world. We all became Ty's caretakers in some form or fashion as he projected his disabled shadow onto the people who loved him the most.

With the onset of Ty's paralysis, a new pattern also came into focus that would eventually be recognizable as a characteristic of Factitious Disorder: fabricated medical relapses that increase in severity over time. You'll recall that Ty first created an explosion in Columbia resulting in a concussion and dislocated shoulder. Then, he created an event in Afghanistan that led to an ER visit with stroke-like symptoms having no root cause. Finally, he created a new handicapped identity requiring a wheelchair. Individuals with Factitious Disorder will often experience symptoms with unclear causes that continue to "level up." Following the pa-

ralysis, there would be other indications of smaller, self-induced injuries usually created as a diversion tactic during personal crises. These injuries and ailments, too, became more exaggerated with time.)

The Fisher House

As a prerequisite of being discharged from BAMC, Ty was assigned a medical advocate to assist us with the next steps. Her timing was perfect because my fear of leaving the hospital had set in. I was terrified and trying not to show it so I could be strong for my husband. The advocate could visibly see our concern and quickly gave us peace of mind. She provided guidance and information and also procured a wheelchair that fit Ty's body type. Most importantly, she secured a room for us at the Fisher House, an on-base residential property situated directly across the street from the BAMC medical center. We could stay there free of charge for the duration of Ty's medical treatments, tests, behavioral medicine, physical therapy (PT), and occupational therapy (OT).

Her finding availability for us at the Fisher House was a miracle. With immeasurable appreciation for everyone at BAMC and especially our medical advocate, Ty and I maneuvered across the street to our new home away from home. As I would learn, the Fisher Houses are more than just a place to stay. They accommodate military and veteran families across the country in some of their darkest hours, serving as both support system and safe haven. From the moment we rolled Ty's wheelchair through the front door to our departure five months later, our Fisher House experience would change our lives forever.

I was lucky not to have to take leave from work during this time. I continued working remotely with the understanding of my executive team, commuting to Austin on Wednesdays only. Ty's boys, on the weeks they were scheduled to stay with him, stayed with Ty's mom instead. These elements of normalcy in a life now full of uncertainty helped to structure our days and keep us going. The other thing that helped, strangely, was the comforting smell of pancakes and syrup, which seemed to infuse all of the Fisher House. Some days the sweet aroma was stronger than others and would last all day long. As I pushed Ty in his wheelchair back and forth from his medical appointments at BAMC to the Fisher House, I would always ask him, "Do you smell pancakes?" We soon learned from the medical staff at BAMC that when the electrical generators at the energy plant on base were running, the air filled with a strong smell of maple syrup. Every time the generators kicked on, the cooling system emitted a vapor that undeniably smelled like pancakes. We thought the explanation was funny. After that, Ty and I often joked with each other: "Do you smell pancakes?"

As the weeks passed, Ty and I discussed many times how fortunate we were that his ailment hadn't occurred two weeks earlier or even the day before it did. The day prior to Ty being driven to the ER by his mother, he'd had his initial Medical Evaluation Board (MEB) review for early military retirement. It had taken him months to get that appointment, and if he'd missed it, who knows how long it would have taken to get another. Two weeks before that was when Ty walked his niece down the aisle at her wedding. How lucky that both Ty's personal and military obligations were fulfilled without fail!

(Looking back, the timing of Ty's paralysis wasn't a coincidence but a convenience. The whole early retirement process was complicated and involved many steps, but suffice it to say the MEB review was an early step, and Ty developing left-side paralysis between it and the next step—the PEB (Physical Evaluation Board) review—would only help his case. In other words, Ty had hemiplegia "just in time" for the PEB and physical examinations. I desperately want to believe that at least some of his ailment was real—that it was not, as the evidence seems to indicate, 100% fabricated from the beginning. If it was made up, then two entire years of my life were based on a theatrical performance.)

Hemiplegia

There were other things to be thankful for—like the fact that Ty's right side, his dominant side, was still fully functional. With his right side alone he could drive a car, write, shave, brush his teeth, etc. It would have been a whole other ballgame if his right side had been paralyzed instead of his left. If the affliction had struck his right side, Ty would've had to relearn how to do most everything with his left side and lost his ability to function independently.

That said, there are daily functions that require both hands to perform and at first Ty needed assistance with these things—tasks like cutting food, tying shoes, buttoning buttons, and zipping zippers. To relearn how to perform these functions, Ty underwent extensive physical and occupational therapy in between a never-ending stream of MRIs, CT scans, EEGs, EKGs, ECGs, spinal tests, nerve tests, behavioral medicine sessions, and general physician appointments. While his functionality improved somewhat, the tests meant to help us understand why he was even in this position remained inconclusive. We saw one neurologist after another and no one could tell us why Ty was experiencing left-side paralysis. I was briefly excited when one neurologist confirmed Ty had hemiplegia. *Finally*, I thought, *a root cause!* Sadly, no. "Hemi" means half and "plegia" means paralysis. He was only confirming that Ty was half-paralyzed. I was immediately deflated.

Permanent hemiplegia is caused by damage to the part of the brain that controls muscle movements. Primary causes are head trauma, stroke, tumor, infection, cerebral palsy, multiple sclerosis, and meningitis. There were no indications of damage to Ty's brain or any of the ailments associated with permanent hemiplegia. Over time, Ty was tested for all of them. Temporary hemiplegia can be caused by a severe migraine, but only lasts twelve to twenty-four hours, at the end of which period full functionality is quickly regained. One neurologist told us that Ty's physical brain was "healthy and immaculate." When anyone asked Ty or me what had caused the paralysis, we just called it hemiplegia since there was no clear way to explain it. That word seemed to satisfy most questions without us having to elaborate on what we basically did not know ourselves. If we could just find a root cause, then we could begin working on a cure. Or, know there wasn't a cure. Either way, not knowing was absolute agony. I prayed for a root cause. It never showed itself.

Like We Belonged There

Fortunately, Ty was able to keep his primary care physician at McWethy Troop Medical Clinic on Fort Sam Houston. This was the doctor assigned to Ty upon his return from Germany. He was a retired major with commendable credentials whose patients included hostages held captive by the Taliban. It was a relief to have this impressive physician continue Ty's care since he was already familiar with Ty and his medical history. Even so, our first visit to his office left a bad taste in my mouth. His bedside manner was abrupt and sarcastic, as if he felt more disgust for Ty than he did empathy. I can still clearly hear his opening words, so appalled was I at what he said. "What's wrong with you now?" he grunted. "Why are you in a wheelchair?" I was inwardly offended by his comments, though Ty laughed it off as if the major was joking. Because his physicians were all high-ranking military officers, I bit my tongue and withheld personal comments but never held back on medical questions. After all, we didn't know what the future held. Ty's paralysis was brand new and we were still scared. How could his doctor be so heartless?

(This specific primary care physician had seen Ty consistently

for multiple reasons prior to his left-side paralysis. I should have noticed his reaction more closely resembled being "put out" than being heartless. Reevaluating the dynamic in the clinic that day, I'd say the doctor's approach was rushed—as if Ty was wasting his time. Again.)

On the flip side, Ty and I became very comfortable at the CPT Jennifer M. Moreno Clinic on base, as we went there three days a week for Ty's physical therapy appointments. Routinely we would take the campus bus from the Fisher House to the clinic. On Wednesdays when I was working in Austin, Ty would take the bus by himself. The driver would use the ADA lift to get him loaded. While Ty was in therapy, I would go down and have a bagel at the coffee shop just down the corridor. The clerk behind the counter and I became friendly acquaintances after a few weeks. She knew exactly what I liked to order, and I knew to the penny what it cost. Physical therapy always left Ty exhausted the remainder of the day. However, he kept a positive attitude despite there being no sign of improvement.

(The amount of time and other resources consumed by Ty's continuous medical testing and follow-up visits to military doctors, VA doctors, and therapists was enormous. It was time and resources Ty stole from deserving soldiers and veterans with real needs. For months, we sat in dozens of military and VA waiting rooms among active-duty soldiers and honorable vets like we belonged there. Now I know we did not.)

Profound Eye-Opener

Our first public outing with paralysis was a profound eye-opener. We had been given a recommendation from a Fisher House volunteer for the best enchiladas in San Antonio. Big fans of Mexican food, we decided to venture out for the first time with the wheelchair and integrate our new handicap into society. Although Ty and I didn't actually talk about it afterward, this excursion proved undoubtedly (to me) how much our lives had transformed.

After I got Ty situated in the front passenger seat, I collapsed the wheelchair and loaded it into the back of the car. It was a bit heavy but I had learned how to use my hip and rotate the chair high enough to swing it into the back with ease. My disbelief that all of this was happening had me going through the motions fairly robotically. Driving out of the medical center, I felt like a new freshman leaving for college. There was excitement and a touch of uncertainty about what lay ahead. We followed the directions to the restaurant and as we got closer to the destination, I realized it was located in what appeared to be a red-light district of San Antonio. Maybe during the daytime the environment was different, but after dark, this location was very unnerving. I checked to make sure the car doors were locked. I remember feeling very aware that my muscle-bound husband could no longer physically protect himself, let alone us, if there was danger. He couldn't even cut his food. I would have to be the person who stepped up and intervened. It was the first time I felt scared that I didn't have what it took to protect us both from harm.

At the restaurant, there was no easy handicapped parking. We parked in the back of the restaurant and took a narrow, gravel-covered path to the sidewalk, which led to the front door. Once we got to the front door, there was no ramp; only stairs. Some men sitting at the bar offered to lift Ty up the stairs. I could tell by the look on his face that he found their offer demeaning. Right as we were opting to find another place to eat, the waiter remembered there was a wooden ramp behind the counter made to retrofit over the stairs. So, we were able to enter the restaurant and order the recommended enchiladas. They were delicious, but not as life-changing as the experience itself. From this adventure, we learned to ask the right questions, and with a little bit of fore-planning, future outings became easier.

Behavioral Medicine

Many weeks after our first outing, Neurology referred Ty to a Traumatic Brain Injury (TBI) specialist. Just like the other neurologists, the TBI specialist could not find anything physically wrong that would cause left-side paralysis. She concluded Ty needed behavioral medicine, suggesting that a multidisciplinary approach involving coping and stress-management skills might help Ty to recover. It was as if she believed he was making the paralysis up and only psychological counseling could help him. I was red-hot with anger. How dare she think Ty was faking! Couldn't she see he was in a wheelchair? As we left the TBI office, I strongly voiced my frustration to Ty regarding her condescending approach and he agreed. "I don't have any PTSD symptoms like most soldiers who have been in combat," he pointed out. Nevertheless, the specialist was insistent and must have held a lot of sway in the hospital because soon enough, Ty was enrolled in a twelve-week behavioral medicine program.

Around the time the behavioral medicine program ended—with Ty showing no signs of improvement physically or mentally—his physical and occupational therapy ceased, too. There'd been no change to Ty's condition, his therapists regretfully informed us. He wasn't gaining any strength or movement or meeting any other indicators of progress. Deaf to my pleas, PT and OT gave us home therapy instructions and sent us on our way. I felt discouraged, as if everyone had given up on my husband. At least we had the option of continuing civilian physical therapy.

(Ty never showed interest in civilian therapy and did not pursue this option during our two-year marriage. The tools for home therapy laid around the house for a while but I never saw Ty actually use them, although he said he did. Eventually, they disappeared and I never saw them again. I accompanied Ty to his very last OT follow-up appointment. The Army colonel over the OT department met with us and asked Ty a series of questions. A few specific questions hit me over the head like a ton of bricks because they caught Ty in two profound lies. First, she asked him what he was doing. He answered by listing off his medical therapies. "No," she clarified, "you misunderstand me. I mean, for employment." Why would she be asking Ty that question if the

Army isn't allowing him to get a job? *I wondered. But of course Ty WAS able to get a job. He had been lying to me all along. Secondly, she asked him if he had gone into theater while stationed in Germany—meaning, had he been sent into warfare or combat in Afghanistan? To my shock, Ty said "no." He could easily lie to family and friends, but he was not about to lie to a decorated military officer in charge of his healthcare.*

Should I have left Ty at this point? Or at the very least confronted him? I should have, but I didn't. Even with the truth hanging between us like a string of flashing lights, I spared him the confrontation because his paralysis was brand new. However, there was no doubt that he had been lying to everyone all along.)

Overcome with compassion for Ty and feeling helpless to do anything for him, I sat in waiting rooms month after month and watched him struggle to use a wheelchair and wondered when life would get better. Not for me, but for him, the man I loved more than anything. I would've walked barefoot across a mile of broken glass if my husband could have regained the use of his left side. The day we received a permanent prescription for a wheelchair was devastating. I didn't know there was such a thing as a prescription for a wheelchair. I thought prescriptions were for drugs only. Before this moment, "permanent" was a reality we had avoided naming. But there it was, on paper. Our last glimmer of hope for improvement had been extinguished.

5

....

HOME AWAY FROM HOME

"Remember us not for what we gave, but for the hardships we helped ease, and for the friendships we helped to form."
—*Zachary Fisher*

With the onset of Ty's paralysis occurring shortly after I'd become his wife, I did my best to support him in every way possible. I'd taken a vow on our wedding day to care of him in sickness and in health, and my whole life I've believed it's important to do what you say. It's something my parents, who have been married for fifty-six years, still model for me. They never leave each other's side, no matter the circumstances, so no way was I leaving Ty's.

Since we'd pretty much exhausted the available repertoire of conventional medical treatments with no improvements or root cause identified, I started searching for alternative methods. I became a Google doctor. I researched everything on neurological function and even integrated brain-healthy foods into our diets. Ty was very good at going along with all of my homeopathic remedies. He ate more flax, chia, and hemp seeds than he probably knew about. I put them in everything from casseroles to tuna salad. I also found an acupuncturist with great recommendations in the Austin area. She was able to accommodate us on Saturday mornings, so we began acupuncture treatments for Ty. This was a pricey out of-pocket-expense for me, but if it yielded any improvement, it was well worth my investment. The acupuncture needles did trigger some visible movement in Ty's left hand and foot. During one acupuncture visit, a twist of the needle made Ty's left hand open wide as if he were giving a high five. These movements were always temporary, though, and eventually acupuncture, too, fell to the wayside. On to the next cure …

During this "experimental" period, we were still living at the Fisher House and attending Ty's follow-up doctor appointments. I always went to as many of them as I could, which was every appointment that didn't fall on a Wednesday. Wednesdays were the only day during the week that I had mandatory strategic meetings at work and had to physically be in the Austin office. It became increasingly frustrating, therefore, when Ty's appointments always seemed to be scheduled for Wednesdays. Every time Ty went to make an appointment, it never failed: The doctors only had Wednesday availability. This was the case throughout our stay at the Fisher House as well as in the years to follow.

(Now, I understand why Ty could only get Wednesday appointments. It had nothing to do with lack of availability on any other day of the week. Ty knew that when I went with him to appointments, I probed and asked questions. I never stopped looking for answers about why this was happening to my husband. Ty must've grown weary of me and passively-aggressively uninvited me to his appointments. I recognized the pattern enough for us to joke about it but didn't understand the deceit behind it until later. Individuals with Factitious Disorder often exhibit reluctance to allow their doctors to meet with family members, friends, or previous doctors. Another box ticked on Ty's Factitious Disorder checklist.)

Adrenaline and Coffee

Daily tasks grew more and more challenging for me between working a full-time corporate job, managing two households, and seeing to it that Ty and his three boys had as much normalcy as possible. I was mentally, physically, and emotionally exhausted, functioning with the assistance of adrenaline and coffee. But more concerning to me than my personal fatigue was the worry I felt for my husband. It's not common for a spouse to become paralyzed shortly after marriage. In my haste to ensure he was getting what he needed (and that my livelihood didn't falter in the meantime), my personality changed. I became harsh and impatient, two very out-of-character qualities for me. I simply did not have time to entertain superficial conversations or social exchanges, not when I barely had time for basic hygiene. Normal everyday dialogue became rushed and forced as the long list of old and new responsibilities swirled around in my head.

Since Ty had no responsibilities other than medical appointments, he became the Fisher House socialite. It was hard not feeling envious that he had time to enjoy himself while I was stuck in our assigned room on conference calls or working on spreadsheets 50+ hours a week. One of us had to ensure there was enough income to cover all the bills, and it wasn't going to be Ty. This was about the time I started to lose my joy. I knew I had a serious undertaking ahead of me if I was to be our sole breadwinner for the rest of our lives, but I had no clear direction on how to manage our new circumstances. I was a new wife to a newly handicapped man, a new stepmom to his three dependent children, and I was newly struggling to keep us all, plus my job, afloat. Meanwhile, I could not forget my own son in college. Even though he was a responsible young adult and took care of things on his own, he still needed me to be available to him. The guilt ran high as my resources ran low. Instead of a newlywed's smile, I wore my stress and my impatience on my sleeve.

My only saving grace during this time was the Fisher House. Before our five-month residence, I had never heard of the organization. Now I describe it to others as being much like the Ronald McDonald House, except instead of serving as an extended-stay residence for the families of critically ill children, the Fisher House exclusively serves military families. It provides temporary housing and community support at no cost to the patients or their families and literally aims to be a home away from home. The bedrooms are set up like master suites complete with attached bathrooms. The common areas resemble cozy living rooms where you feel compelled to take a nap on the couch while watching TV. The shared dining rooms always have fresh pastries and a hot pot of coffee any time you need a boost. Volunteers deliver warm meals on a regular basis or residents can cook in the fully equipped gourmet kitchens. From the moment Ty and I walked through the front door, there was a sense of pure acceptance and camaraderie. The staff and volunteers made us feel as if everything was going to be okay. They truly cared and fought our battle alongside us.

And our battle was a toughie! But, it paled in comparison to the wars other residents were waging. At the Fisher House, we lived among active-duty soldiers, veterans, and their family members recovering from burn trauma, lost limbs, brain injuries, and heart surgeries. Many were fighting for their lives and in excruciating pain as they faced down various terminal illnesses. When Ty and I laid our heads down to sleep at night, I was comforted by the fact that my husband was not in any pain or at risk of losing his life. We were the most fortunate ones in the house, with comparatively the least to worry about.

More Fisher House Stories

Of the countless amazing friendships that came out of the Fisher House, a few stand out. The most heart-wrenching was an active-duty soldier and his wife who arrived shortly after we did. The soldier had been flown into BAMC from Kuwait with a malignant lump on his neck surrounding his vocal cords. He had promptly started treatments for invasive stage-four cancer. They were told the outcome was not favorable and the treatments would be devastating to his body. The couple had two small boys who were being cared for by family members in the far northern States. As we sat at the community dining table learning about each other's circumstances, this soldier mentioned he would be having cancerous nodules removed from his vocal cords the very next morning. More than likely he would lose his ability to ever speak again. I realized I was hearing one of the last vocal conversations that soldier would maybe ever have. My ears were being blessed at that very moment by the sound of his voice. It was highly likely that his two small children would never hear their dad's voice again. It was hard to keep a smile that evening when there was such personal suffering all around us. The underlying pain on his wife's face was very real and stemmed from a deep place. She would more than likely lose her husband within the year. God bless them.

Another resident who impacted me was a heart patient in critical care. This precious little woman was the wife of a deceased military member. She was recovering from open-heart surgery and had months of therapy ahead of her. Amidst her physical pain, she took the time to teach many residents, myself included, the authentic methods for making eggrolls from scratch, just as she had when she was a girl growing up in her native country. Every meal she offered everyone her homemade fried rice, which never had the same ingredients. Her physical heart may have been under repair, but her compassionate heart was as big as the moon. She and her family were with Ty and I during our entire stay at the Fisher House. This friendship remains very strong today.

We all also enjoyed morning conversations over coffee in the communal kitchen. These impromptu gatherings gave residents motivation to get up in the morning, whatever medical challenges they may have been faced with that day. I watched several survival stories and acts of bravery rotate in and out of the Fisher House over a five-month period, including patients from the Center for the Intrepid (CFI) next door. A rehabilitation facility for amputees, CFI taught patients how to walk with their custom-engineered prosthetic legs and use their prosthetic arms for the first time—a real gift to witness. The victories we all shared together as a temporary family were humbling moments, reminding me God is good.

Then there were the selfless volunteers who arrived like clockwork to provide whatever was required on any given day. Sometimes they did the heavy lifting, the cooking, and the cleaning. On other days, they offered comfort with something as simple as their presence and words of encouragement. One sweet couple from San Antonio were ten-year volunteers who came every weekend and would do anything the staff asked of them. They were in their late 60s or early 70s. She was a beautiful woman with a visual impairment who wore the thickest glasses I have ever seen. He walked very cautiously, bent over with a cane. This couple consistently and without fail gave of their time and effort, devoting their weekends to helping the residents of the Fisher House. I'm certain their hearts were full of heartbreaking stories, yet they never faltered or hesitated to be among the suffering and medically challenged. This was the most pure and selfless act I have ever encountered. To this day, I donate monthly to the Fisher House Foundation in their honor. I am committed to this small act of gratitude for the rest of my life.

It was a sad day when Ty and I had to leave the security and comfort of the Fisher House. But, having learned a lot of new skills there, we at the same time felt ready to re-embrace our old life. That life would never look the same again—we would be returning to it for the first time as a handicapped family—but the important things hadn't changed. We had our families and our friends back in Boerne, Texas, and for better or worse, we had each other.

(As Ty's fraud unfolded during the end of our marriage, I thought of the families we'd encountered and the friendships we had made at the Fisher House. It's shameful that through his fraudulent behavior Ty also committed a crime against them. He had no conscience or remorse for being among the deepest of suffering while his intentions were menacing and premeditated. The Fisher House staff, volunteers, donors, and guests did not deserve this fraudulence. Personally, it's hard not to feel guilty for consuming their precious and limited resources even though I was unaware of what Ty was doing.

As I look back at our Fisher House stay, I am eternally grateful to the Fisher House Foundation and the staff for the life lessons

I learned as a temporary resident. The foundation is a topnotch non-profit organization that truly puts incredible effort into making military families feel comforted as they maneuver through medical uncertainty. Even now, I find my thoughts drawn back to the people we met there and the love they showed us. The Fisher House was one of the greatest blessings in my life. I will be forever thankful.)

6

....

RIGHT-SIDE NORMAL

"We do not know until the shell breaks what kind of egg we have been sitting on." —*T.S. Eliot*

As Ty and I got into the routine of our new right-side normal and began learning to live with his paralysis, it became profoundly obvious that society is only moderately set up to accommodate wheelchairs. In the beginning, regular day-to-day activities were complicated not because of the handicap itself, but because in public places simple tasks took twice the effort. Just because establishments are ADA-compliant with handicap parking spots, ramps, and railings doesn't mean adaptations are automatically easy for a disabled person. Sometimes, the handicap parking spots aren't located near the ramp (or there's no ramp at all). Some ramps are so twisty, curvy, and wrap-around that by the time you get from one end to the other, you need to take a break to catch your breath. We felt lucky that Ty was so strong yet, with at least one fully functional side. It could have been so much worse. Even so, we often found ourselves strategically driving around parking lots looking for the best spot for maneuvering Ty's wheelchair, and these spots were not always the designated handicap spots. When they were, I had become so defensive about any "undeserving" person utilizing handicap parking or ADA-compliant seating that I would confront and call out any person who parked or sat in a handicap spot who did not show visible signs of a physical ailment.

(For these confrontations in defense of my husband, I now deeply apologize. My husband was faking a handicap as a disabled veteran. He was "so strong yet" only because he more than likely continued to work out in secret, such that he never developed the type of muscular atrophy you would expect to accompany paralysis. Ty was the most undeserving of all.)

Many retail stores, restaurants, and social venues have narrow sidewalks and aisles. It didn't take us long to realize that eating out was more of a hassle than it was worth. What we had once enjoyed as relaxing and social had become laborious. Most hostesses didn't understand that seating us in the back of a restaurant was difficult not only for Ty and me, but for every table in-between as we wiggled our way to the back. We would typically end up apologizing to people as we maneuvered his wheelchair between the tables and bumped the backs of chairs along the way. We even had several hostesses lead us to a booth. Well, you can't get a wheelchair into a booth. After this happened a few times, I learned to ask for a table close to the front.

For similar reasons, we learned to avoid buffets. With Ty only having the use of his right hand, he wasn't a fan of buffet lines that displayed publicly his lack of independence. I would have to assemble two plates while he followed in the wheelchair behind me. In our earliest dining-out experiences, Ty avoided ordering anything that required me to cut his food. If he could eat it with his right hand using only a fork, that meal would be his first choice. But, this strategy didn't last long. After a while, he ordered whatever he wanted and I would instinctually cut his food when it arrived. Cutting his food, like fixing his plate in a buffet line, was something I never thought about; I just did it.

(While we both apologized when Ty's wheelchair disrupted other people's meals in restaurants, I think Ty savored the attention his disability brought him. For me, it was more about the guilt I felt for inconveniencing others.)

ADA-compliant seating at football stadiums must have been designed by engineers who never had to sit in the first-row aisle for an entire game. It's nearly impossible to watch a football game when you cannot see around the passing crowd who have no other choice but to walk in front of the handicapped seating in order to get to their own seats. Kids and teenagers like to congregate and hang on the railing along the front row. Every five minutes or so, Ty or I would have to tap on someone's shoulder and ask them to please scoot down a bit so we could see the boys play in their school football games. I don't think spectators ever blocked our view intentionally or were purposefully inconsiderate, but their actions always went unrealized and unnoticed until we pointed it out. Stadium ADA seating alienates a handicapped person and forces them to sit in the main walkway or pivot points next to stairways. It may be compliant, but it isn't functional and feels like punishment. Movie-theater ADA seating at ground level isn't any better. After two hours of looking straight up at a giant movie screen, the neck strain also seems like a reprimand for being a handicapped family. Same for establishments without automatic doors. When there were no wheelchair-height buttons to push, Ty learned to pull doors fully open and then back up just enough in his wheelchair to catapult himself through like a sling shot before the door closed behind him.

Finally, we learned how dangerous it could be for Ty to wheel himself across a parking lot without assistance. So low to the ground, like a small child running behind a car, Ty, too, was invisible to cars backing out. There were many close calls where either he or I had to physically bang on the back of a car to get the driver's attention. Otherwise, Ty would have been pinned under a vehicle (or even worse).

Ty at Home

At home, Ty exclusively using his right side became standard for us. After being back in Boerne for several months, Ty grew weary of always sitting in the wheelchair to get around. In turn, he became an expert at maneuvering around the house by standing upright and hopping on or shuffling with his right leg. The boys and I knew that when Ty started to hop from room to room, we needed to steer clear. If he had to stop in mid-hop, he was liable to lose his balance and potentially fall. It became second nature for us to get out of the way when he was on the move between rooms. Ty learned to go upstairs backwards by sitting down on the lower step and using his right arm and leg to pull himself up one step at a time. (This was the same method he used to navigate inclines in the outside world. He would turn his wheelchair around backwards and push with his right leg to get uphill.) Going down the stairs, he would stand upright and hold onto the railing as he cautiously hopped down step by step on his right leg. The more he used his right side to compensate for the loss of his left, he began to have joint irritation and pain. I was worried that if he overused his right side, he could end up having no mobility at all. But, Ty was determined to function independently all day long within the four walls of our home.

Ty being in a wheelchair was only a small inconvenience and became the lesser of two challenges. The bigger obstacle was him not having the use of his left arm or hand. His left arm was flaccid, dangling lifelessly as if hanging by a string. Although Ty insisted on doing as much as he could by himself, there were some things he just could not do. He couldn't cut his food, button buttons, tie his shoes, hammer nails, carry cups and plates without spilling, or do anything else that required the full function of both arms and hands. Before his paralysis, I never thought about the utility of door handles versus door knobs or drawers versus cabinets. Turning a doorknob with one functional hand is much more difficult than pressing down a handle. Pulling out a drawer is much more accessible for a wheelchair-bound person than opening a lower cabinet door that gets in the way and keeps contents out of reach. In other daily tasks, the boys and I learned to fill in the gaps whenever Ty needed assistance. As time passed, it became second nature, something we did without having to think about it.

Ty and I had talked about how wonderful it would be if only he could regain enough strength and function in his left arm to use a cane. Even if he never regained mobility in his left leg, with a cane he wouldn't need a wheelchair and he could be upright all the time. The unsaid, which none of us ever mentioned to Ty, was that if he could use his left arm again, he could also hug us again. Before his paralysis, Ty had been an affectionate hugger, and it secretly broke our hearts not to feel his tight, two-armed hugs. We all unconsciously feared we would never feel one of Ty's hugs again. But, because this was too sad to accept, we all hung onto hope.

(I learned after the annulment that one of the boys had seen Ty use his left arm. Shortly after the onset of his paralysis, Ty was sitting on the couch holding the phone up to his right ear when he

pointed directly at the front door with his left hand and told his son to "close the door." The boy mentioned the incident to a family member immediately after it happened, but it was not shared with me during our marriage.

The one thing Ty could still do independently, even without the use of his left arm, was drive. During our stay at the Fisher House, Ty was not cleared to drive, but back in Boerne he just couldn't stand being cooped up all the time and made the decision to start driving himself. His middle son expressed his concern over this decision. A few weeks later, Ty stated he had been "cleared to drive." However, I never saw any official paperwork to that effect.)

Sex and Intimacy

After Ty's diagnosis, sex and intimacy slowed down to a crawl. Especially while we were temporary residents at the Fisher House, sex was nonexistent. Ty and I openly spoke about this. He said he didn't feel like a "whole man," having just half of a functioning body. And even then, that "function" was limited by Ty's medication. His primary care doctor had put Ty on Topamax to prevent migraines. Topamax is a very potent anticonvulsant drug that made Ty somewhat lethargic and lowered his libido. It didn't help that the walls at the Fisher House were paper-thin. If we could hear people in the adjacent rooms coughing and talking on the phone, we knew they would have been able to hear any intimate moments. Anyway, Ty was rightfully focused on his appointments and therapy. So, I stopped attempting to entice him.

When we got back home, Ty and I had to relearn how to be intimate all over again. The physical dynamic of sex was completely changed as we worked to accommodate Ty's nonfunctional left side. There were times, for example, when his left arm would get pinned between the bed and his torso and he would ask me for help to move it. With practice, he became proficient at using his right side only as leverage during sex and for the purposes of scooting around the bed. After mastering these accommodations, however, Ty found other reasons to put off sex. He'd developed "digestive problems," he told me, that seemed to deter any sexual interest. On the rare occasions when he did feel desire, he would initiate intimacy, so I learned to wait for his prompts and not pressure him. He had enough stress to deal with; I didn't want to add to it.

Eventually, Ty took it upon himself to wean off of his Topamax prescription. As time went by, this did help increase the frequency of our encounters. However, intimacy and frequency never got back to the way they were before his paralysis.

(While the intimacy in our marriage was faltering, Ty's visits, as evidenced by his personal bank transactions, to the erotic full-service massage parlor in San Antonio were becoming more frequent. Was Ty using prostitution as a means to have "normal sex" without having to fake disabled sex with his wife? The erotic parlor owner and provider was subpoenaed and present at our annulment hearing. She made a voluntary statement while seated in the courtroom that her only handicapped client in a

wheelchair was a very old man. That man, she mentioned, was not Ty. It was concluded that even though Ty had frequented this establishment before his paralysis, post-paralysis it became a place where he could temporarily "be himself." Meaning, he was not only paying for sex, he was also paying to be real.

Oh, the irony! As Ty's erotic parlor transactions became more frequent, I gave up the luxury of spa treatments for pedicures, manicures, facials, or massages in order to better balance the budget between two homes. Not that I had time to break away for self-indulgence. Ty meanwhile was quick to boast that he never bought anything for himself, which I believed since he rarely purchased physical items. However, he was spending a lot of money—and government funds at that—on himself in the form of unsavory behind-the-scenes services. Ty was not the financial martyr he claimed after all! And here I'd always wondered where all the ATM cash pulls went and why he was always out of money at the end of the month.

Several times during our more intimate moments, I thought I felt Ty's left hand briefly grab my hip. I quickly dismissed the sensation, thinking I must have brushed up against him. Now I know he really did grab my hip with his left hand. It wasn't just my imagination.)

Disability Compensation

The day finally came for Ty's appointment at the Frank M. Tejeda VA Clinic. The VA doctor assigned to Ty would perform an intensive physical exam and evaluate Ty's previous medical records to determine "how disabled" Ty was. Ty would be given a percentage rating that would determine his disability compensation. The appointment required driving to San Antonio first thing in the morning, and we were told the appointment would likely last until lunch. That was no problem as I was accustomed to lengthy stays in clinic waiting rooms. We arrived a little early and the doors were still locked, so we waited in the car for a while. Ty was nervous about what the morning would bring but glad that another milestone would be behind him.

When the doors were opened, I found this particular VA clinic made waiting as comfortable as possible with the Military Order of the Purple Heart organization providing free donuts and coffee to all soldiers and veterans waiting for care. Ty signed in at the front desk and the nurses quickly called him back for the start of his four-hour allotted exam time. Midmorning, Ty wheeled out to the waiting room for a short break and we shared some coffee and donuts. Then, he went back to complete the second half of the exam. As noontime approached, Ty's VA doctor came out to the waiting area asking for Ty's wife. My anxiety briefly skyrocketed as I assumed something must be wrong. I was relieved to learn Ty was only asking for some assistance getting dressed and putting his shoes back on. The doctor led me back to the examination room and I helped Ty put on his socks, pants, and shoes. Another VA appointment was behind us; now it was time to wait for the results.

(The day at the Frank M. Tejeda VA clinic made me suspicious,

but I quickly dismissed my doubts and didn't entertain them again until after the annulment hearing. Specifically, I'd found it very odd that the VA doctor had asked me to help Ty get dressed. At the time, Ty was dressing himself every day with no issue. Why on that day had Ty needed assistance? I now believe that Ty used me, his wife, as a sympathetic prop—one more tool for convincing his doctor to give him a 100% disability rating ... which he received. In the days, months, and years that followed, Ty went back to dressing himself; just not on that specific day during that specific appointment.

Ty was adamant about not having pictures taken of him in his wheelchair. At any family event, social outing, or other photo opportunity he would insist that he stand up in the photos with the wheelchair out of sight. This hadn't been the case when we were living at the Fisher House or when we attended social events at the Warrior and Family Support Center (WFSC) on base. Then, it was just the opposite: Every picture we have with our friends at the Fisher House or WFSC shows Ty sitting in the wheelchair. It was only once we got home and among family and friends that he insisted on standing up for photos. Two perceptions for two new bubbles. On the military base, completely helpless. With family and friends, the effort to be independent.)

Over the next year, Ty worked diligently with both the VA and the SSA to receive additional disability compensation. His baseline percentage had already been approved, but for reasons I didn't understand, it appeared (from the outside, anyway) to be an uphill battle to add ailments not included in the baseline rating. Month after month, Ty sent e-mails, made phone calls, and went to appointments, all in an effort to get what he deserved. I'd come home from work and ask him how his day was, and his answer was always the same: "Sent some emails. Made some phone calls." Watching his constant struggle, I began to understand why there are so many stories in the news about how challenging it is to navigate the VA system. I was seeing firsthand the energy it takes for veterans to get administrative attention and funding. For Ty, chasing down his benefits had become the equivalent of a full-time job. I fully supported Ty and frequently voiced my concern over how hard he was having to work, but since I had no access to any internal military websites or even the Tricare insurance plan through the Defense Enrollment Eligibility Reporting System (DEERS), my hands were tied when it came to helping Ty, a paralyzed veteran, fight for what the government owed him.

(At the end of our marriage, Ty was receiving $4,900 per month in VA disability compensation and $1,900 in SSI benefits from the Social Security Administration. His total tax-free government benefit was over $6,800 per month. Ty spent almost two years working to increase his disability compensation by adding physical ailments to his baseline assessment. All of his e-mails, phone calls, and appointments were to add hearing loss, peripheral vision loss, and urinary and bowel incontinence among other complaints. As I was thinking my husband was being treated

unfairly by the VA, he was really working the system. In addition to the monthly $6,800 disability compensation, he received a $20,000 VA automobile grant (not for an adaptive vehicle, but simply to buy a new car), approval for an $80,000 VA housing grant (meant for adaptive improvements), $20,000+ in VA vocational rehabilitation classes, and some custom pieces of high-tech electronic equipment and ergonomic office furniture. Before my abrupt exit, he was working on getting a power-assist wheelchair with a self-propelling feature. Ironically, he had requested this new custom wheelchair be red since that's my favorite color. Ty was conning the federal government right under my nose.)

Tapatio Springs Hill Country Resort

Apartment living with two very active boys (Ty's oldest son by this time was away attending college) and a handicapped husband in a wheelchair was proving to be incredibly difficult. As the first year's apartment lease neared its end, we decided to search for a more spacious rental house. It was 2016, though, and home leases were averaging 40% more than mortgages on comparable properties. Rather than "throw money away" on leasing then, our intention was to pool my corporate salary and Ty's steady flow of VA retirement and disability benefits to buy a house instead. Our search led us to a one-level house with a xeriscaped lot that required no lawn maintenance. It had just one small step up from the garage into the house and non-slip tile flooring, making it easy for Ty to maneuver and perfect for our situation. Best of all, it was tucked away in a tranquil corner of a golf resort community called Tapatio Springs, six miles west of Boerne. We made a fair offer and it was accepted the same day. The mortgage process began.

Later that day, the broker called me to verify our social security numbers. Our credit scores, he said, were coming in guardrail-to-guardrail—a Texan phrase meaning *from one extreme to another*, like a car bouncing between guardrails. My score was abnormally high in the 800s and Ty's was abnormally low in the 500s. After verifying that our numbers were correct, the broker informed me Ty was not a candidate for a conventional loan. Moreover, he didn't even meet the lowest credit threshold for a VA loan. If we were to proceed with the mortgage and purchase the house, I would have to do so solely on my financial merit and at my risk.

During a lengthy conversation, Ty explained his rock-bottom credit score as a "residual effect" of the financial devastation caused by his divorce. Because the Army had never paid him his back-pay and he'd never gotten another job, his credit score had never rebounded. Feeling sorry for Ty, I decided to finance the Boerne home on my own even though I already had another mortgage on my Austin house. It was doable financially, but emotionally it sucked, as it put all the risk and burden on my back. Even so, the decision was made. The apartment was not conducive for school-age boys and a handicapped man in a wheelchair. We had to move forward into a house with more space. I closed on the house in mid-summer and we were settled before the boys started school that fall.

(While I was securing a mortgage loan so Ty and his boys would have a house, Ty stole several pieces of diamond jewelry from my Austin home and pawned my personal property in Boerne, Texas. The jewelry theft amounted to more than $6,000—felony value. During this same timeframe, additional erotic full-service transactions were building on Ty's personal bank statements. I was unaware of any of it.

Narcissists are pathological liars and always have plausible excuses for their bad behavior. Ty consistently blamed other people for his debt and rock-bottom credit score. He persisted in claiming that his ex-wife had left him financially devastated, the Army cost-center debacle had cost him his salary and backpay, the Incapacitation Board (INCAP) "didn't care about" his ailment, and that his left-side paralysis prevented him from obtaining a civilian job. Ty always had an excuse. He was never at fault.

For the record, I had frequently and forcefully "encouraged," and sometimes outright demanded, that Ty find a job. He told me he was looking, but if he ever did, he never landed an interview.)

Several months passed in our new home—a better situation, it turned out, for everyone but me. Unable to achieve anything that looked remotely like balance, I was beginning to unravel. Being a new resident in an unfamiliar town with my family and friends hours away only added to my distress. Ty's family was there for me, but I was still becoming very isolated very fast. There were days when I didn't recognize myself due to the utter lack of sleep and complete exhaustion. Managing two households, working a full-time corporate job, commuting between two cities, keeping up with Ty's medical appointments, and caring for my stepchildren among other family responsibilities finally became too much. The days bled together as I found myself working evenings and weekends so I wouldn't fall behind on the job that provided for our livelihood. But that meant a to-do list that never got done and missing several of the boys' sporting events, which filled me with guilt. More than that, it drove a wedge between us, resulting in some discipline problems.

The scenario usually went like this. I'd ask the boys to do something, and they would ignore me or talk back. Being the stepparent, I wouldn't feel I had the "authority" to correct Ty's sons, so I'd go to Ty instead. Ty would either dismiss my concerns as "normal adolescent behavior" or promise to talk to the boys himself. These "talks" always took place on the way to school in the morning, and as Ty was the one who drove the boys, I have no idea if any such talking ever happened. Their behavior certainly didn't change. Soon, I started to lose my impulse control. Where I'd always been patient and had a long fuse, I became quickly ignitable at any sign of disrespect from the boys and even sometimes from Ty. We may have unpacked our moving boxes and brought order to our new home, but our lives were spiraling into uncontrolled disorder.

7

....

ALARM BELLS

"The recognition of confusion is itself a form of clarity."
—T.K.V. Desikackar

The patterns of narcissistic behavior evident before our marriage were primarily limited to love bombing. They were all positive behaviors meant to create the illusion of happiness and to secure devotion. After the onset of Ty's left-side paralysis, different types of narcissistic behavior emerged, almost all of them negative and designed to control. The change in Ty's personality was so drastic that at times, I wondered if he was becoming depressed. It made sense, I thought. Losing one's mobility could do that to a person. And there were the signs. Whereas Ty had previously shown pride in himself by dressing sharply when out and about in public places, now he only wore warmups, athletic bottoms, and T-shirts. His choice of daily attire started to closely resemble pajamas. He also began laying down for frequent afternoon naps as he ran out of energy in the middle of the day. If I was working remotely from home using the office area in our bedroom, he would typically lay his head back on the couch and close his eyes for about an hour. Whether this was depression or just laziness, I couldn't tell. His attitude, meanwhile, became ever more arrogant, as if Ty thought he was superior to everyone around him. I was perplexed and unsure how to cope with this change as I was at the same time going through my own transition to our new normal.

Testing My Theory

The more time Ty spent as a handicapped person, the more, too, he seemed to savor being recognized and honored as a disabled veteran. When we were out in public places, he would field admiration from complete strangers especially if he was wearing his Army T-shirts or jacket. I learned Ty preferred not just to be a "regular" disabled person in public. He had to be recognized as a disabled Army veteran. More often than not, he would be approached by people commenting, "Thank you for your service" or "We appreciate your sacrifice for our country." When dining out at restaurants, we frequently had our meals paid for by patrons who preferred to stay anonymous. At the end of our meal, the check would be brought to our table already paid in full. Every time this happened, Ty appeared to be modestly annoyed by the kind gesture; but then again, he never failed to advertise by putting on his Army T-shirts or jacket before we left the house. It was almost like he had celebrity status being a disabled Army vet in a wheelchair.

After I noticed this obsessive desire of Ty's, I tested my theory. Ty had an appointment at the Audy Murphy VA Hospital in San Antonio one afternoon. While he was showering, I put his Army jacket and all of his Army T-shirts in the bottom of the laundry basket. I then went about my business and forgot I had done this until the panic began. Like a teenage girl looking for her favorite jeans before a date, Ty was frantic to find his Army jacket. I told him it was eighty degrees outside and he didn't need it. If he thought he would be cold in the medical facility, he could just grab another jacket from the coat closet. No, Ty said. It had to be that jacket. He even called his mother to see if he had left it at her house. He eventually found the jacket all crumpled up in the bottom of the laundry basket and wore it to his appointment. This behavior was a sign to me that something was terribly wrong. Ty not only knew exactly how to draw attention and field admiration for his ailment, but he liked it.

Ty once asked me while we were out shopping if it embarrassed me when he asked retail clerks if they had a military discount. Personally, I believe that all active and retired military members should get discounts across the board, no matter where they shop. In Ty's case, though, it seemed to be less about the discount, which we didn't actually need, and more about the praise that being recognized as a disabled vet earned him. Guaranteed 100% of the time the clerk wouldn't just give Ty a simple yes or no, but their response would always be followed by "Thank you for your service." Ty craved these accolades, not the monetary concession.

The Pharmacy

Manila envelopes from the VA started arriving in the mail like Christmas cards. Every week or so there would be a new delivery with a variety of medications. They seemed to auto-ship on regular schedules. The deliveries became so frequent we dedicated an entire shelf in our master bathroom linen closet to these VA medications, which we jokingly referred to as "the pharmacy." Soon, orange pill bottles were stacked two deep. To the endless stock of pain relievers, muscle relaxers, allergy pills, nose sprays, narcotics, sleep aids, nausea medications, migraine tablets, urinary bladder control prescriptions, and other VA medications, I personally added a few bottles of holistic vitamins and supplements from the health food store. Although Ty rarely took any of the medication, it kept coming in abundance and like clockwork. There were times when I would take a sleep aid or allergy medicine as needed. If the boys had a sports injury, Ty would dole out a muscle relaxer or pain reliever on occasion. Ty's mother benefited the most from "the pharmacy." Since she had severe arthritis and constant back pain, Ty passed along to her his prescription for Naproxen. His sister sometimes took the prescription for Tramadol. Almost anything anyone in the family needed could be found in our bathroom linen closet.

Funding Ty's Lifestyle

Ty's odd behavior and odder decision-making continued. A longtime good friend of Ty's in the auto business offered him a part-time desk job answering phones where responsibilities were not physically tasking. He and his wife needed a little help with administrative functions and thought it would be good for Ty to make some money and feel productive in society again. I thought this would be a wonderful first step toward reentering the civilian workforce and was certain Ty would jump at the offer. He declined, even though he had no reason to turn it down. He was filling his days with simple household tasks of no consequence or real value. I didn't press Ty on why he'd declined the offer because at the time, his disability was still fairly new. Perhaps he needed more time to prepare himself emotionally for going back to work as a handicapped person.

Months later, someone in my high-tech professional network asked for Ty's resume so they could help him get a remote work-from-home position that would be perfect for his condition. I pestered Ty for his résumé for almost a year, during which time he showed no interest. In the four years we were together, Ty never sent out one single résumé nor looked for any kind of job. Before we were married, he'd had the excuse of being caught between Army cost centers and not being allowed to work. During our marriage, he'd become left-side paralyzed, which had hindered and delayed his job search. As we got beyond the medical hurdles, though, Ty's excuses were running out. His lack of effort started to puzzle me. I work with many highly skilled and intelligent handicapped people in the corporate world. My company is continually rated by Disability Equality Index (DEI) as a top supporter in the workplace. Ty's disability was no reason not to work. But then, he had no reason *to* work, either, as his monthly VA and SSA disability deposits were the equivalent of a healthy paycheck. Ty even called the two days a month these deposits arrived "paydays." In reality, that money *was* wages earned—by other Americans whose taxes were funding Ty's lifestyle.

Memory Like a Steel Trap

As I became increasingly exhausted from working and trying to balance everything new, I was convinced I had become very forgetful and absentminded. Ty and I would have conversations that by the following day I had completely forgotten. Ty was adamant he had told me about specific things—appointments, schedule changes, meal plans, whatever—but I had no recollection of either the discussion or its conclusion. How could I be so neglectful and forgetful? My memory had always been like a steel trap. I felt as if lack of sleep and the long to-do list were impacting my ability to remember events and conversations. Ty's baffled reactions to my inability to recollect decisions we had made together made me feel guilty and in some cases confused. Often, the decisions we had made were not routes I typically would have chosen. But since I had already previously agreed to the plan, I was committed. Ty always seemed to be two steps ahead of me with our personal plans.

Luckily, my forgetfulness had not yet drifted over into my job. I seemed to be able to recall discussions and schedules at work with no issue. Thank goodness the voids in my memory had no negative career impact.

(Narcissists use gaslighting as a form of manipulation. Gaslighting convinces a victim they are forgetful or absentminded, causing the victim to doubt themselves and believe what the narcissist says. In this way, the narcissist can persuade the victim they said something they didn't really say or twist their words to effect a specific outcome, either by paraphrasing comments out of context or by referencing conversations that never occurred. They may use reproachful responses like "I told you that," "we talked about this," or "you already agreed." Some textbooks and articles refer to this technique as a "word salad" intended to keep the victim off-balance. During my marriage to Ty, I did not recognize the gaslighting as it was happening to me. I simply felt like I was in a constant state of confusion.)

Ironically, the more we settled into our new house, the more I felt like a guest in my own home—the home that I had bought. There was a strong sense that I alone was now on the outside looking in. Decisions were being made without my input as if I was no longer a contributor. I was learning of family events from external sources rather than from my own husband. Any time I expressed my distress about this dynamic change, Ty listened to my concern and acknowledged the problem. He agreed with me and promised to work on shifting the paradigm. Over time, his promises proved empty. No actions backed up his words, or else he would do the exact opposite of what he'd offered. My instinct was to blame myself. Had I done something to change how he and the boys felt about me? No, Ty assured me, everything was fine. But "fine" looked like being squeezed out of my own life, the life I had built and financed for the people I loved.

(When a narcissist accomplishes their goal, becomes bored, or feels challenged by their victim, the narcissist may devalue and even discard their supply, thinking it's no longer needed. They will push their victim to the side with no remorse as if they are invisible. The shift is not subtle, though it can look that way from the outside. Not all narcissists are physically or verbally abusive. They don't always come across like a freight train. Some are calm, collected, never raise their voice, and can manipulate you with the precision of a surgeon. They can be sweetly condescending while slowly destroying you with coercive control. They may seem so rational and "put together" that you start to believe you're the irrational one.)

Every once in a while, I'd still dare to make a suggestion. It was usually something simple, like about what we should do on a Saturday afternoon. No matter how straightforward my suggestion seemed to me, Ty would find a way to make it harder and more complex than necessary, until what seemed like common sense would end up convoluted. If I pointed this out to Ty, he would tell me, "I may not get to the end the same way you do, but I still get to the end." These pronouncements would be followed by a lecture with no room for two-way conversation. When I or one of the boys tried to interject, he would talk over us with an elevated tone. Should I direct a question to the boys, Ty would answer for them before they could speak. After a while, it seemed that Ty was the only person doing all the talking.

And that's all it was—talking, endlessly, about nothing. Rarely would he give me a straight answer to a direct question. Everything was ambiguous. I experienced this throughout our four years together, but it got ridiculous the last year. I had become conditioned over time to ask Ty only yes or no questions. If he couldn't give me a clear yes or a clear no, then I knew to assume he was either not telling me the truth, dodging, or trying to think of a quick explanation. His standard go-to responses to most of my questions were "I got this," "Trust me, I'll take care of it," or "I've got it all squared away." Those were not answers. They were only fillers to pacify. He had an effortless ability to come up with plausible excuses at the drop of a hat. But that's all they were—excuses—such that I became suspect of almost every response.

(A narcissist will never answer your questions honestly. Instead, they act "put out" or attack you for pestering them. They will try to escape being questioned at all costs. Their tactic is to steer conversations by shifting and deflecting to another topic. This is a trick they use to evade the truth without actually having to think up a quick lie. They deliver ambiguous replies and answers

with no content. Like gaslighting, non-answers and silence are a form of manipulation. At times, they may "drown you out" or talk over you to get you to back off. More often than not, a narcissist's answers leave you more confused than before you asked the question.)

Quirks of Body Language

I began recognizing Ty's giveaways, the little quirks of body language that indicated he was lying (or, in the process of creating a real-time lie in his head as he was talking). The most profound tell was his rapid eye blinking while explaining something. His eyelids would blink so fast that they became small slits and all I could see were the whites of his eyes. The first time I saw this rapid eye movement was the day we met. I remember thinking to myself back then, *Ty keeps getting something stuck in his eye! Poor guy!* The eye blinking was so vigorous that even my friend Sandy noticed it during a few conversations with Ty. Sandy also said she'd thought he had something in his eye and almost wanted to offer him some eye drops. This rapid eye blinking only happened when he was talking. It never happened any other time or when other people were speaking. One of his sons made a comment once during dinner that he could always tell when his dad was lying because he would "blink." Bingo! I wasn't the only person to recognize what behavior—lying—led to Ty's unusual body language.

Another physical indicator of Ty's lying was the profoundly long inhale that happened any time he said something untrue. He would inhale through his nose only, in a manner abnormally long and excessive. It occurred during face-to-face conversations and could be heard over the phone as well. I recognized this trait later on in our relationship after experiencing it too many times. *Deep long nose inhale = lie.*

(Liars tend to blink rapidly because lying is stressful and they become nervous. They blink obsessively when they are in the process of constructing or inventing a story in their mind. Their eyes are the giveaway. Also, when someone is lying, their breathing patterns change. Nervousness and tension cause the liar's heart rate and blood flow to change, in turn causing the liar to be out of breath. Ty's friends and family members admitted to noticing his excessive inhales as well as his blinking.)

Ty's third and most unsettling habitual response were these uncomfortable, bone-chilling stares. I noticed this tendency early on in our relationship, but it really came to a head post-paralysis. He would lock on to someone or something with an unwavering stare at the oddest times. It was very awkward and menacing. There were moments when I would be driving the car and Ty would stare at me from the passenger seat, knowing I couldn't look back at him or take my eyes off the road. When this would happen, there would be no conversation, only silence. I could see him staring at me in my peripheral vision. The stare wasn't angry, just a blank, emotionless, penetrating gaze. Once, I asked Ty to stop staring at me when I was driving. He reacted defensively, saying, "What?! It's not okay for a husband to look at his beautiful wife?" He quickly turned my simple request into something that made me feel guilty for asking. However, he didn't do it again after that day.

He also stared at the boys, mostly when they were watching TV. "Dad," one son would say, "stop staring at me. It's creepy." That's when I knew I was not the only person who'd noticed Ty's unnerving stare. Thank goodness. I wasn't crazy or being overly sensitive after all. The boys were right: It was creepy. I wouldn't wish Ty's stare on anyone.

(The first time I read about "the narcissist's predatory stare" was after the annulment. I was flabbergasted. This empty and hollow stare, which both the boys and I had experienced, is a real thing! It's commonly used by narcissists to intimidate and size up their victims like prey. The stare is almost reptilian, certainly primal in nature, and has been described as dead, dark, or seductive. It's usually a prelude to self-gratification of some form.)

So, my husband's behavior was changing, but one important thing had stayed the same. No matter how much he blinked, stared, and/or lied, he kept up with the sweet, romantic gestures. They didn't stop even though Ty had some physical challenges now and was experiencing mood changes. For example, not one morning went by that Ty didn't have a hot cup of coffee ready for me when I woke up. He would bring me my favorite things when he was out and about running errands, stopping at the local bakery for a pastry, swinging through a drive-through for an ice cream treat, or picking up a bouquet of flowers on his way home. Despite facing cruel physical challenges each day, Ty never faltered in showing me that he loved me. His dismissals, although becoming more frequent, didn't measure up to all of the affectionately generous ways he proved he loved me. I never questioned Ty's love for me so I did my best to let his strange behaviors roll off my back.

(Narcissists use gifts and compliments to cover up and draw emotional attention away from what's really happening in the background. Gift-giving is typically nothing of substantial value but frequent enough to foster obedience from the victim. Narcissists give out of fear and from their need to continue the game.)

8

....

POCKET FULL OF LIES

"Whoever walks in integrity walks securely, but whoever takes crooked paths will be found out." —Proverbs 10:9

Our Tapatio Springs home was nestled in the valley of a golf resort community between several rolling hills. The elevated front porch overlooked the golf course with several greens in clear view as well as the surrounding ponds. We could watch golfers play and hear the ping of a golf ball when the head of a driver hit it just right. The golfers' voices sometimes echoed through the valley, bouncing off the hills like a megaphone. Unbeknownst to them, nothing they said during their golf game was secret. We would occasionally hear a curse word or two from an unhappy golfer or constructive criticism being offered from a fellow player. Some mornings on the front porch with a hot cup of coffee were very entertaining.

The location of our house was in a tranquil spot along the back side of the golf course. Getting there required a six-mile drive down a beautiful, twisty road on which various species of wildlife, including rabbits, deer, raccoons, wild turkeys, skunks, hogs, and snakes, liked to make appearances day or night. Tapatio Springs didn't have streetlights, meaning at night, the world was pitch black. This made the stars so profoundly bright that some evenings it felt as if we could reach out and touch them. I loved our little corner of the universe. How could I know it was about to blow up in my face?

Fraud Discovery #1 – Financial

Several months after I closed on the house and we were completely settled, the mortgage broker sent a package with some residual documents from the file. Our latest credit reports were included. Even though I knew the aggregate scores for both, I skimmed through the details anyway. My jaw dropped at what I saw. According to the report, Ty had four accounts that had gone to collection and he had recently been approved for a brand-new AAFES Military Star credit card that already had a substantial balance. I'd been shocked by his lack of financial transparency during our first tax return debacle, and again when I'd found out what his credit score was. Now this too? Had I been aware of Ty's new account or that more of his accounts had gone to collection, there's no way in hell I would have made the decision to finance a second house all on my own. This was now the third major financial surprise that Ty had been hiding from me, all of which I'd discovered on my own or through other sources—not from my husband.

Thank goodness I was working at the corporate office in Austin when I saw this credit report for the first time. I was too emotionally charged to speak to Ty directly. So, I wrote him a strongly phrased, fact-based e-mail telling him that when I got back to Boerne on Sunday, I wanted to talk about the financial "surprises" plus a few other things—namely, his refusal to get a job and the differences between our parenting styles, which were becoming more obvious as the boys' disciplinary issues continued. I scheduled a date and time for the conversation, outlined the agenda, and even gave him a couple of days to digest and prepare for the meeting, same as I would any business associate. (To be honest, I also needed the time to calm down.) This wasn't my first rodeo with Ty, but it was the first time I felt compelled to grab the bull by the horns.

Sunday afternoon rolled around, and we spent hours talking at the kitchen table about every bullet point on my list. I appreciated Ty's thoroughness, though he was also quick to let me know he didn't appreciate my email's tone or what he felt were the many "unfair accusations" I'd made. First, he was adamant that the new AAFES credit card on his credit report did not belong to him. He insisted it was fraudulent activity. Someone must have stolen his social security number, he said, opened the account, and charged a very large amount. He promised he would call the company the next morning and clear it up. "Okay," I told Ty, "but I want to be on that call with you." Let's say someone *had* stolen his social security number. We'd need to know what steps to take next to prevent other forms of identity theft. Ty was incredulous. "What?" he exclaimed. "You don't believe me? Why do you need to be on the call?" I wanted to believe Ty, but something didn't seem right. He was more defensive than concerned that his personal information may have been hijacked. Finally, I wore him down and he agreed I could be on the call.

The following morning, Ty took the boys to school and I took the opportunity to peek inside his coveted backpack. This backpack carried his laptop as well as his military and medical documents and it normally went everywhere with Ty. I was surprised he'd left the house without it. In all our years together, I'd respected Ty enough never to look inside it. But that morning while he was away, I dove right in and completely violated my husband's privacy. Given this latest financial surprise, I wanted to know exactly what was in that backpack. I unzipped the front pocket and pulled out handfuls of unopened mail. Some of the envelopes were six months old. Most had scary red alerts: PAST DUE; OPEN IMMEDIATELY; FINAL NOTICE. This mail was not addressed to our home but to his mother's address. It's why I didn't know about any of his accounts going to collection.

I completely emptied the front pocket of the backpack, ripped open all the envelopes, and started organizing the account statements into categories. I spread these documents all over the bed in our master bedroom so I could see them all. There were too many to fit on our kitchen table. That's when I found it: the new AAFES credit card statement for the account he'd said was fraudulently opened under his social security number. The AAFES statements detailed transactions for items purchased at the commissary on base at Fort Sam Houston, items that were now in our home. This was the moment I knew Ty had a real problem—not only with financial nondisclosure and massive debt accumulation, but also blatant lying. He'd lied about this new credit card and made up another lie on top of it.

Why hadn't Ty just told the truth? I'd given him two days to think about how to delicately come clean. But instead, he'd purposefully and with graceful ease looked me in the eye and lied to my face. I realized that if he could lie big, then he could lie small. I had suspected falsehoods, white lies, and exaggerations in the past. But now, I wondered if everything I had previously dismissed was also untrue. I'd literally found a pocket full of lies.

While muddling through the documents I had spread out and categorized all over the bed, I heard the garage door open. Ty pulled up in the driveway, came in the house, went to the kitchen, made me a fresh cup of coffee, and came into our bedroom to give it to me. Unfortunately, I was already beyond furious. I went crazy out of my mind and transformed into a hysterical woman having a screaming fit. I took the cup of coffee and threw it in the bathroom sink. As words spewed out of my mouth, I remember thinking to myself, *I can't believe I have such rage pouring out of me.* It was uncontrollable and unstoppable. I don't think there had ever been a time in my life that I'd had so much uncontainable fury. I must have screamed "YOU'RE A FUCKING LIAR!" a hundred times until my throat was raw. Those were the only words I could muster, and at the same time, the only words that expressed the truth. I wanted Ty out of the house, stat. But, we had custody of the boys that week and they would have had no place to go had I kicked Ty out. So, I grabbed some things and drove to the Austin house. Ty didn't stop me.

Good as Stolen

I had previously kept Ty's financial misdeeds to myself and had not shared my concern with family members or friends. This new chunk of financial deception, however, directly impacted my bottom line and my investments and put me at very high risk. I'd worked all my life as a single mom to build financial security and plan for my retirement. Now it looked as though my decisions had been purely for Ty's benefit and to my detriment. Beside myself and as a last resort, I finally reached out to my parents for emotional support and explained the reasons I had stormed out. Ty's actions constituted a serious form of financial infidelity, they said, not to mention all the lying and secret-keeping and mail-hiding. A few days later, my parents came to Austin to help me work through my financial concerns and my crumbling marriage. I no longer trusted Ty. He told lies. Big lies. Little lies. Lots of lies.

I showed my parents Ty's financial statements as well as the credit reports. I told them about Ty's truck being repossessed (the one he'd said was stolen), the accounts he'd stopped paying on the month we got married (the ones that had since gone to collection), the surprise IRS and government debt that had been taken out of our tax return, the rock bottom credit score, the massive credit card debt, and the new credit card he had opened without my knowledge. I was particularly distraught about one specific account that had gone to collection. It was for his purchase of the black leather sectional in our living room. Ty had purchased it on credit and never made one single payment. In my mind, the leather sectional sitting in my living room was as good as stolen.

My parents were shocked by the debt and defaults. And, that Ty had covered it up and lied about it for years. My parents loved Ty and thought a lot of him. They were very concerned yet supportive of us resolving this problem. After all, it was just money. If money can fix the issue, then it's no big deal. However, this issue was bigger than money. Bigger, even, than my marriage. I couldn't trust my husband, but more than that, I couldn't trust myself. I'd been blind to his faults and believed him for so long. Why had Ty deceived me like that? And how had I let him? In a family discussion (without Ty), my parents and I came to the conclusion that the best solution was two-fold: financial counseling and marriage counseling. It would take time to rebuild my trust in Ty and in us, but in the meantime, if he would just come clean and be honest with me, we could at least start to rebuild his credit. We invited Ty's mother to join what amounted to a financial intervention.

(Ty's mom must have seen the past-due notices arriving at her address. Ty couldn't have intercepted the mail every day. Yet, in

all that time, she never said anything or gave his mail to me to
bring home. She only gave it to Ty.)

The five of us—me, Ty, my parents, and Ty's mom—sat down
to dinner in our Tapatio Springs home. Four of us knew why we
there; only Ty was none the wiser. As we ate, we made casual conversation. I don't remember it feeling forced, though I was plenty nervous. At the point I would have normally started clearing
plates, I broached the topic. Something light, like, "So, we got the
craziest thing in the mail the other day." Once Ty realized what
I was talking about, he became uneasy—but also, to his credit,
non-combative. He readily agreed when my parents suggested
marital and financial counseling. The only strange thing he said
was, "I never bring my work home," which initially confused all of
us because Ty didn't have a job. "Well," my mom said, "Dee brings
her work home." And I did sometimes on nights and weekends.
"I mean I don't bring my *work* home," Ty repeated. "You know,
my combat stories. I don't burden the family with everything I've
been through." It didn't fit the conversation, but I understood the
point Ty was trying to make, the card he was trying one more time
to play. He was the disabled Army combat veteran. No one could
trump that. As if to prove it, he stood up and hopped outside on
one leg.

Later, I watched Ty through the living room window. He was
sitting on the patio staring at the full moon. I was relieved not to
be the object of his "narcissist's stare" at that moment, and relieved,
too, that I'd spoken up. I was no longer alone with Ty's lies. My

parents would go on to be, as they've always been, an incredible support system. Ty's mom said nothing that night, not to me or to Ty, and she never would.

Marriage Counseling Begins

Ty took it upon himself to find a local marriage counselor. My only request was that he or she be faith-based. Ty found a counselor who fit the criteria. Unfortunately, the counselor's schedule was fully booked until after the first of the year, which was a few months away. So, we had to wait until January to start counseling. In the meantime, Ty and I created a strict budget and opened a joint checking account just for household bills. This would allow us both to monitor our household spending. I also took the initiative as Ty's wife to have all of his mail forwarded from his mother's house to our residence. No more hiding mail.

The holidays came and went, and it was the end of December. I asked Ty if the marriage counselor had responded to him about scheduling an appointment. Ty said he was still booked. This frustrated me because I wanted at least to get on this counselor's schedule, or else find another counselor who could accommodate us. So, I independently sent the counselor an e-mail asking for his availability. He replied to me within the hour and said he had an open time slot the following week. This was not the information Ty had conveyed. I booked the appointment and our faith-based marriage counseling journey began.

I was hopeful that counseling would resolve the financial torpedoes that kept exploding at my feet and help me regain my trust in Ty. I really struggled with the years of deceit but was convinced that Ty and I could get back on track. Trust is the foundation of any relationship, whether it's a friendship or a marriage. If I didn't regain my trust in Ty, I felt I would have to move on. And then what would people think of me? Would I be perceived by the Boerne community as a ruthless woman who'd married a healthy, strong man only to abandon him as soon as he'd become handicapped? No one from the outside looking in would see the reality that my husband was continually lying, accumulating massive amounts of undisclosed debt, and keeping financial secrets. They would only see a heartless woman who'd left her helpless husband when he needed her the most. This fact weighed heavy on my heart. As I shared my thoughts with my friend Sandy, she was quick to tell me, "If this marriage isn't right for you, no one who loves you will judge you." I knew she was right. I am a good person. But I didn't want to be perceived negatively, even if the audience knew nothing about me.

On one particularly hard afternoon, I opened up over lunch to another longtime close friend, Stephanie. Just like Sandy, her advice was the same. She pointed out that I needed to approach the repair of my marriage with love, but at the same time, not fall prey to naïvety. "You should keep a log book," she suggested, "documenting timelines and anomalies. I've always thought Ty appeared to be a good guy, but sometimes things aren't what they seem." Stephanie lived close to Boerne in the San Antonio area and back in the day had been my college roommate and sorority sister. She had known me for over thirty years. And, after living with me for a few years, she had a heightened ability to read between the lines when I was speaking. Seeing in my face my desperation to fix my marriage, she urged me not to throw caution to the wind. "There's clearly something more profound going on behind the scenes to make Ty hold onto his grandiose lies for so long," she stressed. I absorbed her words of wisdom and became more alert.

Marriage counseling began—and with it, another outlet for Ty's excuses. Fifteen minutes or less into each counseling session, Ty would shift the discussion away from our trust issues and directly to his disability, which would then consume the rest of our time together. By making statements like, "Put yourself in my shoes," or "How would you feel if you had to wake up like this every day?" he deflected from our real problems and dominated the conversation. To my frustration, the therapist allowed this behavior, letting Ty use his physical ailment over and over again as justification for his bad behaviors. It felt imbalanced, like the therapist was in Ty's corner. (And who wasn't, most of the time? Ty was that good at charming people!) Had I been more knowledgeable about the process, I would have looked for a different therapist. Having never gone to couples therapy before, however, I let it go, assuming this must be "what therapists do."

(After he saw video footage of Ty walking across the garage floor, the therapist admitted he'd missed the signs of narcissistic personality disorder.)

Real Relief

I never expected a perfect marriage—not even close—but I did expect a healthy marriage. A healthy marriage, to me, is one not plagued by trust issues, lying, secrets, deceit, and dismissal. Since couples therapy wasn't helping, I began to think my marriage was in dire straits. Only when our therapist suggested we try individual counseling—as in, Ty and I would meet with him separately, at different times—did I find any real relief. I'd hoped we could work through our issues as husband and wife, but as it turned out, I had some of my own issues to work through first.

For the first time in my life, I was emotionally on edge and suffering from noticeable anxiety. The anxiety was not due to Ty's paralysis. Accommodating his handicap was the easy part, a daily route adjustment. No, my severe stress came from the daily ambiguity. Never knowing what was going on in my marriage had changed my temperament from confident to confused. I had developed high blood pressure and extreme fatigue. On the occasions when my elevated blood pressure further spiked, it caused the fine blood vessels in my eyes to burst. I was resorting to taking sleeping aids from the second-shelf pharmacy in order to rest at night. Emotionally and physically, I no longer recognized myself.

("Losing yourself" is a common experience among victims of narcissists. Narcissists make you forget who you once were, and you literally become unrecognizable to yourself. Victims tend to set aside their basic needs and desires, sacrificing their emotional

and physical wellbeing to please and take care of the narcissist. As a result, they may develop serious health issues they did not have prior to life with the narcissist. I knew these things were beginning to happen to me; I just didn't know why.)

During individual sessions, the therapist helped me to find myself again. It was good that he knew Ty and was also working with him because I didn't have to explain Ty's actions or personality; the therapist had seen it firsthand. Later, this faith-based counselor would be with me through every step of the fraud discovery, providing clarity and spiritual guidance as the ominous thunder approached from a distance. He would support me as the storm surrounded me and as I walked through the path of destruction it left behind. The therapist, I realize now, was never intended for my marriage at all; all along, he was only intended for me. Sometimes God gives you what you need even though it may not be what you want. I wanted Ty. I wanted my marriage. But they weren't meant for me.

9

....

JUST ENOUGH ROPE

"Life in real time is messy. The fingerprints of God are often invisible until you look at them in the rearview mirror."
—Levi Lusko

After we started marriage counseling, Ty began acting even odder than usual. What was meant to help me regain my trust in and respect for Ty caused him to construct higher walls and throw up thicker smokescreens. Rather than being more transparent and honest, he became even more secretive, evasive, and distant. He acted as if his financial secrets were my fault because I had found them, and further, as if I was looking for an immediate exit when the opposite was true. I wanted nothing more than to work through our challenges so we could move past them. In response, Ty started doing bizarre things that made no sense … which was when I met the Ty who lived beneath the surface.

(A narcissist's greatest fear is being exposed for who they really are. When they feel backed into a corner or feel you're onto them, they begin to scramble for a new defense. When they begin to lose emotional control, they quickly look for a way out. This is why marriage counseling with a narcissist is a futile effort. They don't want resolution and repair. They want to escape without being discovered.)

Advance Warnings

One afternoon before the boys got out of school for the day, a tense situation arose between Ty and his ex-wife. She was clearly upset at Ty and sent him a series of very abrupt text messages. Out of angst, Ty let me read the string of communication. Yes, her words were very angry, but what really caught my attention was one specific sentence: "You should be ashamed of yourself, always living off a woman." Normally, I wouldn't have thought much about it, but with all the financial discoveries rising to the top, her words spoke loudly and directly to me. Was she aware of what was happening inside our marriage because she had already lived it? It was the first time I'd ever wanted to call and talk to her. But, I refrained. I was determined to make my marriage work because I loved my husband. Running to Ty's nemesis for information would have guaranteed failure and the end of my marriage.

(Do not close your eyes to the narcissist's signs. Trust your gut instinct. Recognize love bombing for what it really is. I tried to fix a marriage that was built on pretense from the very beginning. Our marriage was doomed before it even started.)

Stranger than the text exchange with Ty's ex-wife were the times I would come home from working in Austin to find tasks done around the house that were impossible for Ty to do on his own without the use of two arms and hands. These were things like hanging pictures on the wall and folding clothes. "How did you do that?" I would ask. "Did your mom come over and help you?" No, Ty would tell me, he'd done it himself. "It just takes me longer, but I can figure things out on my own." I would smile and thank him, even as I was convinced that his mom was coming over while I was away. I thought she'd been doing it for years and he just didn't want to admit it. Part of the reason I thought this was because Ty always made it a point to check what time I was leaving Austin for my drive back to Boerne. At first it had seemed like a protective way of making sure I got home safely, but after a while I realized it was his "advance warning" for what time I would be walking through the door—leaving his mom enough time, perhaps, to skedaddle.

Stranger still was when Ty started giving me "advance warnings," letting me know, for example, that he wouldn't be available to answer his phone between certain hours of the day because he planned on taking a nap. Ty often took naps, but he'd never "preplanned" them before. This new scheduled nap time really baffled me until I accidentally found out what Ty was using the allotted hour for. Some days traffic would be lighter than expected and I'd arrive home early to see Ty either talking or typing furiously on the phone. Sometimes he'd be in the house and sometimes he'd be sitting in the car a ways up the road, like he was hiding. He wasn't scheduling naps, I realized, he was scheduling calls. But why and with whom? And how come the messages he sent to these mysterious recipients were long—paragraph after full paragraph—when his texts to me were always necessarily short? I got single sentences or even one-word replies because it was hard for Ty to type with his right hand only. But, sitting next to him on the couch, I could see him writing novels to other people. I just couldn't see what they said. (I'm blind as a bat without my reading glasses.) "Who are you texting?" I'd ask him innocently. "Mom," he'd say. "Who were you talking to earlier?" "Mom," again.

(Who was Ty talking to and texting? I never did find out. It could have been his mom; they were close. Later on, I thought maybe he was talking to the contractors or inspectors trying to get that $80,000 home allowance for disabled vets. Or maybe he was making appointments with the massage parlor? I really don't know. Whoever he was communicating with, he definitely didn't want me to know about it.)

Ty took two measures to make sure I didn't intercept his calls or texts. First, he kept his phone alerts on silent so I wouldn't know when anything new was coming in. Second, he began "booby-trapping" his devices. Fully aware now that I would breach the unspoken rule of not messing with his things, he began strategically placing coins or trinkets on top of his laptop, tablet, and phone. He would also stack books or papers on top of his backpack so he could tell if I'd been snooping or meddling. In therapy, I was vocalizing my concerns regarding Ty's dishonesty, and at home, Ty was being more covert than ever, actively attempting to disguise or otherwise prevent me from accessing his sensitive data. When it came to disciplining the boys, Ty always told me, "I give them just enough rope to cross the line. Then, I pull their rope back for full control." Ty was pulling my rope back.

The Break-In

One weekend when the boys were at their mom's house, Ty and I decided to spend the weekend in Austin. Knowing we would be gone, Ty's middle son and four of his teenage friends picked the lock on the exterior garage door at the Tapatio Springs house and spent Saturday night there unsupervised. With all of Ty's narcotics in "the pharmacy" and for a million other reasons, this was a really bad move on his son's part that prompted me to install a home security system. Against Ty's wishes, I bought the most comprehensive package, consisting of interior and exterior motion-sensitive cameras. Ty didn't like being "watched" in our own home, but since the house was vacant on occasional weekends and it was in my name, I insisted for the safety of the boys and our home that we install cameras.

It didn't take long for Ty to find a way to refute me. Whenever I drove to Austin for work, he would physically unplug the interior security cameras (of which there were three—kitchen, living room, and hallway) and completely disconnect them from the network. I knew he was doing this because the app on my phone would go offline. It would have been easier for him (and more covert) to just hit the off button, but he always went to the extra trouble. By the time I returned home from Austin, the cameras would be plugged back into the outlets and connected to the network. I found this behavior curious, but never said anything to Ty about it.

(In the end, the break-in incident was a blessing. Without this unfortunate event, there wouldn't have been a reason for me to install home security cameras in the house. By extension, I might never have discovered Ty's fraud nor had the evidence to initiate a federal investigation. Ty's son breaking in was the golden key that turned the chain reaction. Divine intervention!)

Bathroom Commotion

The doors! Ty began closing layers of doors behind him as he moved throughout the house. If he was shuffling on his right side from the main living area to the master bedroom, he would shut all the doors in between after he'd passed through them. If I needed to talk to him, there would be several barriers of doors I would have to go through to get to him. It was as if he wanted to be able to hear

me coming and know exactly where I was as I moved from room to room. This interesting new behavior was not subtle and very noticeable. Even when I was in the bedroom alone, he would intentionally come close the door. Several times I asked Ty to leave the bedroom door open, but he told me he was trying to "conserve energy." I never understood the logic behind his strange explanation.

A very heated argument one afternoon prompted me to threaten that I would "put a for sale sign in front of the house." Long story short, I had spent all weekend washing and folding laundry for myself, Ty, and the boys—including many loads dedicated solely to their sporting activities—and placed the laundry in their rooms, asking them to please put it away. Ty's middle son assured me had before he left to go hang out with friends, but the next day, I found his clean clothes crammed in the laundry basket and mixed in with his dirty clothes. Furious, I told Ty to ground his son and he refused. "That's it!" I screamed. "I've had enough!" I was financially supporting Ty and his kids, cleaning up after them, managing two houses, and working a full-time corporate job, yet Ty had zero respect for the life I'd given them. That's when I threatened to sell the house—to which Ty, predictably, had no response, leaving our conflict unresolved.

Now that we weren't speaking to each other, I went to the master bedroom to work at the desk and Ty went to take a shower. Five minutes later, he opened the bathroom door with a towel around his waist and asked if I could come help him. Once in the bathroom, I saw the top cabinet drawer was laying on the floor. When I looked up to ask Ty what had happened, I could see a very large goose egg on his forehead, as swollen as if a golf ball had been lodged beneath his skin. He explained that he had slipped, hit his head on the edge of the drawer, and the drawer had fallen to the floor.

Processing the bathroom environment, I thought it didn't make sense. I'd been working only feet away from the bathroom door and had never heard any noise or commotion—certainly not the bang as my husband, the drawer, and all of its contents went crashing to the ground. The drawer itself was deeply hinged and would've had to have been opened all the way to the edge of the rail to come free. Even then, it would have taken an extremely strong force. There should have been damage to more than just Ty's forehead. I think what confused me the most was that the drawer lay neatly on the floor with all of the toiletries still organized. It looked as if it had been unhinged, removed from the cabinet, and placed methodically on the floor. *He totally injured himself on purpose*, I marveled. What other explanation could there be? The crime scene didn't fit the crime in the least.

I shuffled Ty to the couch so he could lay his head back and I grabbed an icepack. While the bump on his forehead was swelling and starting to bruise, he was insistent that he didn't need to go to urgent care. As I was getting him comfortable with the icepack, I couldn't stop thinking, *Oh my God, he hurt himself. He actually hurt himself.* Feeling confused, I returned to the bathroom, picked up the drawer, and slid it back into the cabinet.

(During the early stages of the private investigation and prior to the annulment, I asked the private investigator to find out if there was any history or indication of Ty ever hurting himself. I was so bothered by the event in the bathroom that day, it was something I just personally needed to know. What I saw did not match what I'd heard. While the PI was unable to turn up anything concrete, I strongly believe this episode was a symptom of Ty's Factitious Disorder. The forehead injury swiftly distracted my attention away from our argument and replaced it with sympathy—Ty's favorite tool.)

Power Grabs

After my middle stepson turned sixteen and gained his driver's license, he began to drive himself to school using Ty's vehicle.

Since I worked remotely from home, my car was always available in case Ty or I needed to go anywhere. Ty would typically have his morning coffee, shower mid-morning, get dressed, and leave the house while I was on my daily conference calls. In the beginning, I thought Ty was trying to be courteous and allow me to work with no distractions. Maybe he was going to visit his mother. But there were days when Ty would leave and be gone for five to six hours. Short errands seemed to take all day. One day he mentioned he was running to the grocery store and topping the car off with gas. He was gone for hours and came home with one gallon of milk from the convenience store on the corner and an empty tank of gas. These long daily absences made no sense and in the meantime, left me stranded at the house six miles outside of the Boerne city limits.

What I think now is that leaving me stranded was a power grab and a way to "put me in my place," because soon, Ty started encouraging the boys to do the same. Before I'd discovered his financial deceit, he would take my side in arguments over the boys, at least promising to talk to them even if he didn't actually do it. After my discovery, Ty stopped pretending, period. He made it clear it was three (he and the boys) against one (me). He supported whatever they wanted to do while dismissing or ignoring my concerns. The boys learned they could get anything they asked for from Ty even if it wasn't in their (or our) best interest. If I bought the boys a gift, Ty would tell them it was from him. Ty didn't care about being a real parent. He cared about being the popular parent. He cared about the control this gave him over all of our lives. I was sometimes experiencing dual manipulation: mature, sophisticated manipulation tactics and immature ones all at the same time.

(After the annulment hearing, I learned that Ty's middle son was aware Ty had repeatedly lied to me over the course of our four-year relationship. This child was holding Ty's secrets over his head as a bartering mechanism. He allegedly said to one family member, "I have Dad's balls in my hands." When this information was conveyed to me, so many past events began to make perfect sense. Many arguments between Ty and I had stemmed from what I felt was his children's full control over him. I'd thought it was because Ty was too lenient and a pushover, but that wasn't the reason at all. My manipulator had been manipulated—and by a child.

Regarding Ty's son: No one knows whether narcissism is "nature" or "nurture." Might it be genetic? Or can narcissism be modeled and learned? I've read everything I can on the subject and have had in-depth conversations with many therapists about this question. The professionals all have their opinions, but science has yet to take a hard stance one way or another.)

Ty began sleeping on the couch most of the time. He made me believe this was out of courtesy for me. I'm a light sleeper so he told me he didn't want his snoring to keep me awake all night. Most evenings I tried to coax Ty to bed but after a while, I just stopped. He seemed to enjoy staying up to watch TV or Netflix on his tablet.

I once overheard him tell one of the boys that the reason he was sleeping on the couch was because "Dee has insomnia." Well, that wasn't true at all. Even though Ty continued to show me affection in the form of words and gifts, our days were becoming separate and now our nights were as well. Ty's side of the bed grew empty and cold between the sheets. The vacancy sold to me as a "courtesy" felt more like a punishment ... though for what, I didn't know.

(Up until I discovered Ty's visits to the erotic full-service massage parlor, I felt guilty for being a light sleeper, as if I'd asked Ty to sleep on the couch when I definitely hadn't. I wanted the comfort of sleeping with my husband. After learning about his frequent visits, I was more than relieved he was sleeping on the couch of his own accord.)

Unnerving Conversations

Unbidden and out of the blue, Ty would say the most bizarre things. They seemed planned, not spontaneous, and intended to achieve specific effects. One instance left me feeling somewhat threatened, while others felt more like Ty was trying to sow discord, goading me into saying things he could later use against me.

As I was in the master bathroom one evening getting ready to go out to dinner, Ty came in and sat down on the edge of the bathtub. His conversation starter was, "Sometimes I worry about myself." *Hmm.* "Are you feeling okay?" I asked. He told me how all the men in his family had a history of violence, that they were prone to physical confrontation when provoked. His paternal grandfather, he said, had killed a man. His dad had once become so angry he'd almost beaten a man to death. "I hope I haven't inherited that tendency," Ty mused. Feeling as if I'd just been indirectly threatened, but unsure if that's what Ty had meant to do, I said, "You shouldn't worry, honey. There's a lot of dilution in the gene pool between you and them." With that, Ty exited the bathroom as quickly as he had come in. I was left very uneasy, recalling past conversations about violence with Ty.

When we first started dating, Ty told me he had physically threatened a man by putting a gun to his head in a parking lot. The man, who Ty accused of "not leaving his family alone," was so terrified he had peed himself. Another time, Ty told me he could make his ex-wife "go away" (and make it look like an accident) because he "knew people who knew people." But, he clarified, he could never bring himself to do it because she was the boys' mother. These conversations should have made me turn and run, fast. But at that point in our relationship, Ty's love bombing and emotional manipulation already had me hopelessly addicted. In my victim's eyes of pure devotion, he could do or say nothing wrong.

A few of our disagreements and conversations Ty twisted so badly that when he repeated back to me what he thought I had said, it came out completely differently. One evening I was so tired from commuting back and forth to Austin that I mentioned the drive home had felt like being on autopilot. I barely remembered driving from point A to point B. "I'm worried," I said, "that if I get in autopilot mode and get drowsy, I could veer off the road into a ditch. Then again," I added, "*if* that happened, it would be okay because I have faith I'll meet my Maker." Somehow, Ty took from this conversation that I was suicidal. "What?" I asked, shocked. "That's not what I said." "You said you felt like ending your life," he (incorrectly) paraphrased back to me. No! This wasn't a discussion about suicide. It was me explaining to my husband that I was exhausted from driving back and forth between two cities. In his head, he had completely changed the meaning of our conversation.

Another misinterpretation left me even more distraught. During a heated discussion about the boys' consistent disrespect and bad behavior, I strongly expressed my concern that Ty was way too lenient and that his dismissal of my feelings was causing strife between me and his kids. This evaluation had nothing to do with the boys but everything to do with Ty. To this day, I still cannot believe how Ty regurgitated my feelings. "So, you hate them," Ty said. After I pulled my jaw off the floor, I abruptly replied, "No! You dismiss the concerns of your wife for the wants of your children. They seem to have complete control over you." Ty just shrugged. "I heard you say that you hate them."

(Ty twisted my words to make me seem emotionally unstable and unreasonable. By re-packaging old conversations in new ways, he made me look like a suicidal woman who hated his boys—boys I loved. These conversations confused me and made me wonder what Ty's endgame was. This was gaslighting at its very best.)

In the midst of Ty's undesirable behavior changes, there was one welcome new activity that was music to my ears. Ty mentioned that while I was in the Austin office, he had begun working out with the boys' high school football coach. I was pleased to hear he had once again taken an interest in physical conditioning. The two years we spent dating, working out had been a priority for Ty. It was a standard daily activity that came as naturally to him as eating, breathing, and sleeping. Since the onset of his paralysis, he had shown no interest in working out or physical therapy. He wouldn't even consider a chiropractor. Ty's new adoption of some physical and social activity was very good news. Finally, a glimmer of progress.

10

···

THE UNDERNEATH

"Call to me and I will answer you and will tell you great and hidden things that you have not known." —Jeremiah 22:33

Another tax season rolled around. It was time for our second joint tax return as a married couple. Since the first joint tax return had proven to be a nightmare full of revelation and non-disclosures, I was rightfully nervous. Ty assured me there would be no more hidden transactions this time. Thank goodness! I had already had too many financial surprises over the past two years. Surely, there were no more.

I gathered all the tax documents and only needed Ty's personal checking account statements to finish itemizing our sales tax, which I do every year. Ty made me request them several times before he gave them to me. When he did, the statements looked like an Area 51 government cover-up. There were black Sharpie lines through most of the transactions. The document was 80% redacted. I was speechless for a moment. "That's to prevent any confusion," Ty offered. "I blacked out the transactions that can't be itemized." *Does he think I'm a total idiot?!* I wondered. I knew what transactions were itemize-able. After all, I have a bachelor's degree in Business and work a corporate job managing millions of dollars on a daily basis. It must have taken Ty hours to draw black lines through all of those pages. I took what was visible from his statements and completed our joint tax return. In early March, we got our full tax return deposited with no surprises this time. I was relieved that Ty had been truthful.

Fraud Discovery #2 – Prostitution

Our IRS refund safely in the bank, it was time to put our tax documents away in the filing cabinet. As I was organizing all of the documents in a folder, I had a gnawing urge to look through Ty's redacted personal bank statements one more time before those black Sharpie'd statements were filed away forever. I started with January and went through the months page by page. By holding them up to the light, I could clearly see the transactions he had crossed out. On October's statement, I saw a blacked-out transaction to a day spa in San Antonio. I thought that was kind of strange since we have a resort spa two minutes down the hill

THE UNDERNEATH

```
DEBITS
......AMOUNT.TRANSACTION DESCRIPTION
     8.98 POS DEBIT                110516
          WALGREENS STORE 1223 S   BOERNE
    15.10 DEBIT CARD PURCHASE      110616
          AMC  ONLINE #9640        888-440-4262
    26.46 POS DEBIT                110616
          MURPHY7652ATWALMART      BOERNE
          ████████████████████████████████
          ████████████████████████████████
          LUNCH MONEY NOW          210-496-2877
    60.88 POS DEBIT                110616
          HEB  #621420 WEST BANDERABOERNE
          ████████████████████████████████
          JEFFERSONBK371 N. MAIN STBOERNE
          ████████████████████████████████
          GVTC                     800-367-4882
          ████████████████████████████████
          SWBC MORTGAGE     LOAN PAYMT *********
    63.56 POS DEBIT                110816
          Wal-Mart Super Center1126BOERNE
          ████████████████████████████████
          ████████████████████████████████
          DELTA DENTAL      NOV 16 EFT *********
          ████████████████████████████████
          TOLL/MSB 888-811-4565    800-5687004
          ████████████████████████████████
          TOLL/MSB 888-811-4565    800-5687004
          ████████████████████████████████
          249537101 IH 10 FRONTA   BOERNE
    46.72 DEBIT CARD PURCHASE      110916
          CHUY S IH-10             SAN ANTONIO
    52.96 POS DEBIT                111016
          WM SUPERCENTERWal-Mart SuBOERNE
     4.79 DEBIT CARD PURCHASE      110916
          PICO-JOHN'S ROAD         BOERNE
     5.40 DEBIT CARD PURCHASE      111216
          PICO-JOHN'S ROAD         BOERNE
          ████████████████████████████████ 6
          BOERNE EXPRESS WAS       SAN ANTONIO
```

from our house and we get a discount for being resort members. I skimmed past the transaction and moved on to November and December, where I found many more day spa transactions. *Weird.* Ty had never mentioned going to get massages in San Antonio, almost an hour's drive away in congested traffic. Why was he driving so far? That's when I looked up the day spa and everything changed. After digging deep, I realized it was an erotic massage parlor located close to the San Antonio airport.

I spent hours that night combing through the reviews for the erotic massage parlor. I had to pay for access, which alone made me feel disgusting. I couldn't believe what I was seeing and reading. The place was a rub-n-tugger's dream. It not only offered low-level happy endings and blow jobs, but the majority of the reviews were for full-service sex. I learned that, on average, service providers made an extra $160-$200 in tips per session. I was in denial at first that this establishment was the same place on Ty's statements, but the statements showed a clear pattern: Month after month, Ty would gas up the car in Boerne, pull $200 cash from an ATM, then charge a "spa service" to his card. I could draw only one conclusion. Ty was paying for full-service prostitution at an erotic massage parlor posing as a legitimate day spa. I collapsed, an emotional mess barely able to breathe through the tears. Our marriage was already on thin ice, but it came to an abrupt end that night.

No self-respecting woman (or man) would continue a marriage based on lies, secrecy, and now, infidelity. Unable to sleep after my latest discovery, I lay in bed running through every scenarios. *What am I going to do now? Do I confront Ty? Do I wait until after I talk to an attorney? Do I act like everything is normal? OMG, what do I do?* As a million questions circled in my head, I had an even worse thought. *What if Ty's activity isn't new? For how long has he been seeing prostitutes?* I realized Ty's personal bank statements from our first joint tax return the previous year were also in the filing cabinet. I jumped out of bed, pulled them from their folder, and started skimming through them as fast as I could. There it was! Again, and again, and again. Ty was a regular. There were transactions from before and during our marriage. The transaction on April 20, 2015—the day after we returned from our honeymoon—literally brought me to my knees. As I stared at the date, I understood Ty had never intended to keep the wedding vows we'd made to each other only one week prior. He'd married me for what I could provide for him and his boys. With a large inheritance eventually coming my way, I had been used as supply from the beginning in what might have been, had Ty succeeded, the world's longest con.

The following day I sent a screenshot of the erotic parlor's exterior to my friend Stephanie. She lived and worked in San Antonio and as such, was very familiar with its neighborhoods. I texted her one simple question, "What do you see in this picture?" Her two-word response came immediately. "Happy ending." She knew nothing about my motives or the fact that I'd been up all night researching this place and digging through bank transactions. But, she didn't need to. The picture said it all. Her innocent response was the validation I needed to begin my search for an attorney.

It was two weeks before I could get a consultation with an attorney to discuss my findings. Since I kept hoping there was a really good explanation for years of covert spa transactions, I parked outside of the establishment one afternoon and watched as men only rotated in and out for several hours. The parlor had bars on its windows and security cameras around the perimeter. A city bus stop let people off out front; the adjacent parking lot was for semi-trucks. Across the street, homeless people begged for money outside a pharmacy until they moved to the Mexican food place next door. I just had to see it with my own eyes. After my "bird on a wire" investigation, I opted not to confront Ty. I was having a hard time emotionally accepting and digesting the facts. I could not imagine my husband going into an unsavory place like that to pay for sexual gratification. It physically made me ill. On top of the infidelity, he'd put me at risk for whatever STIs he might have contracted. Later that week, I would go and get tested, but that day, I went home and acted as if nothing was wrong. Only I knew my time as Ty's wife was over.

(The private investigator would later confirm that the parlor required clients to wear condoms. There was some relief in that news, but still …)

Electric Pain

During my two weeks of pretending and waiting to meet with an attorney, I further educated myself on Ty's erotic establishment of choice. While he stayed up late and slept on the couch, I used my phone to read the parlor's advertisements on rubads.com, adultlook.com, redmassage.com, and backpage.com and do related research. Who knew "teeth whitening" was erotic code for a blow job? Or that the acronym FS meant *full-service sex*? I learned a lot about how erotic establishments operate and ride the legal line, and more about the stranger in the next room I called my husband. Before my attorney ever hired a private investigator, I became a novice investigator. All I found were monsters hiding in the dark corners of my life with Ty.

As a result of all the pretending (really, how *did* Ty do it?), I started having severe tension headaches. These headaches were so painful I could barely function or even hold a thought. Every day they got progressively worse until bright lights and loud sounds became unbearable and the persistent headaches turned to solid, twenty-four-hour migraines. No over-the-counter medication helped. Sleep was my only (temporary) relief.

One Saturday morning I woke up with severe pain shooting across the right side of my head. This new pain was electric, and it made the migraine underneath seem insignificant. I couldn't turn my head from side to side or look up and down without wanting to scream bloody murder. I limped from the bedroom to the kitchen and told Ty I might need to go to the emergency room. First, though, I wanted to sit on the couch for a minute to see if the shooting pain would stop. Ty made me a cup of coffee and placed a heating pad on the back of my neck. It did nothing to soothe the excruciating pain, which was getting worse. It was clear that I needed medical attention, so Ty drove me to the hospital.

I don't remember getting out of the car or walking through the ER entrance. But, I do remember sitting in triage thinking, *I'm going to die. This must be a stroke.* The shooting electric pain was so severe I wanted the debilitating migraines back. The ER nurses ushered us to a room and started some initial testing. Then they left Ty and me to sit quietly and wait for the doctor. Ty got up out of his wheelchair and hopped over on his right leg to sit on the bed next to me. He grabbed my hand and said, "I wish it was me instead of you. I would trade places with you in a second." Unbeknownst to him, he was the reason I was in the ER in the first place. He'd caused the stress headaches. What irony.

At that moment, I wanted to tell Ty everything I knew about his stealthy trips to MacArthur Avenue, but I held steady. The doctor came in and within five minutes he'd diagnosed me with occipital neuralgia. In essence, extreme muscle tension in the base of my skull had trapped and pinched nerves, causing the electric shooting pain. To relieve my agony, the doctor instructed the nurse to give me two injections in the base of my skull. I'm fearful of needles but welcomed these injections. They couldn't stick them in me fast enough. When they didn't help, I begged for more. After additional injections in the base of my skull, I was feeling some relief. I was discharged with medication to keep the pain from coming back, and referred to a neurologist for further diagnosis. This neurologist would order a series of MRIs to find the root cause, and I would go along with it. But of course I already knew the root cause—Ty.

Missing

As my marriage was starting to turn upside down, my friend Sandy traveled to Boerne from the Texas panhandle on a business trip. We met for dinner and I told her everything I had discovered about Ty's financial fraud. There was so much to fill her in on, I never got around to mentioning the erotic full-service parlor. In the car driving back to my house after dinner, she looked at me and said, "What else?" She instinctually knew the financial deception was not the whole story. Since we had been closely connected from early childhood like sisters, she could tell just by being in my presence that there was more. Because I couldn't explain the infidelity without a flood of tears, I let her read a drafted letter I had written to Ty. I physically saw her blood pressure rise as she read it, and then our conversation ran the course of the entire evening. With characteristic empathy, Sandy listened to my poignant discovery. Her trip was a blessing that had come at exactly the right time.

At some point during our conversation, I mentioned unrelated to anything else that my one-karat diamond ring was missing. "The last time I had it was at the Austin house," I said. "Maybe the carpet-cleaning service or a repair contractor took it?" Without hesitating and with strong conviction, Sandy leaned toward me and said, "Ty stole your jewelry." I shook my head, unwilling to believe her. Ty wouldn't do something like that. But my friend persisted: "I'm telling you, he took your ring and hocked it." On the off-chance she was right, I promised not to take my wedding ring off my finger, lest it go missing too.

Cut off at the Knees

Finally, I had my appointment with the attorney in San Antonio. He'd come highly recommended with solid credentials, including years of experience in family law and a proven record of success. Since Stephanie lived in the area, she accompanied me to the consultation. She knew I was about to embark on a very big challenge and she wanted to be there to support me. I appreciated this gesture as I was about to step into the unknown. Stephanie had done some independent research, too, even driving down to observe Ty's erotic establishment herself. She was also 100% sure the parlor offered unsavory activity behind closed doors. As we walked into the attorney's office carrying every document outlining Ty's defaulted accounts, massive debts, and massage parlor transactions, plus print-outs of the erotic establishment's web links and sexual reviews, I felt well-organized and prepared. With Stephanie's help and this attorney's expertise, surely my case would be a shoo-in. We'd fly through the legal proceedings, my marriage would be over, and everything would be okay again like it was before I'd found out my husband was a liar and a cheat.

The consultation left me feeling like I had already lost. According to the attorney, Texas is a no-fault state—meaning that when it comes to divorce, both spouses have to agree they don't want to be married anymore. Neither has to prove the other is guilty of any misconduct. Even with all the evidence I had, the attorney said, a judge would be more likely to rule in Ty's favor than mine, simply because of how pro-military San Antonio and the surrounding areas are. The court would see a disabled vet with two school-aged children and decide Ty deserved more sympathy than me. It was even possible, this attorney added, that Ty could be granted temporary living arrangements to stay in the house I had bought. Discouraged, I paid the consultation fee and left.

Back in the car, Stephanie commiserated with me. She, too, had been taken aback by the attorney's quick assumptions of defeat. We agreed the primary takeaway was that Ty's status as a disabled veteran cut me off at the knees before I could get started. "You are a strong woman," Stephanie told me. "You need a second opinion." So began the search for another attorney.

This time, I looked outside the city of San Antonio in the more rural communities for someone who might be familiar with the Boerne county judge. Divine guidance pointed me to the perfect attorney. Fifteen minutes into my initial consultation, she said point-blank, "This is pure fraud. You can get an annulment based on fraud." As she explained it, outside of Ty's financial non-disclosures, it was clear he'd had no intention of keeping our wedding vows. The fact that he'd visited an erotic full-service massage parlor for sex the day after we came back from our honeymoon made him a fraud. His fraud entitled me to "undo" our marriage as if it had never existed. The word "divorce" was never used again. She was hired!

"I suggest you file for annulment right away at the courthouse," my new queen-in-shining-armor said, "but hold off on serving Ty until I can get a private investigator to gain an affidavit from the parlor." If she could do that, we would have hard proof and not just circumstantial evidence that the establishment was indeed prostituting full-service erotic activity. It would take her some time to achieve. "In the meantime," she advised, "go home and act as if everything is normal. Keep up your normal day-to-day routine with Ty and the boys." She was asking me to become my husband—a full-time pretender.

Fraud Discovery #3 – Misrepresented Military Career

Another wink from God: The private investigator my attorney hired just happened to be a retired Army officer! He had served our country in various military capacities over a span of twenty years and like Ty, had a service-related disability. The PI quickly discovered another unexpected surprise. In addition to everything else he'd falsified, Ty had also been misrepresenting his military history and rank. His Texas Army National Guard separation-from-service paperwork listed his ending rank as SGT E5. There was no indication of Ty ever having completed the training for or having earned the rank of Army Warrant officer. He'd served as military police during his eight years in the Air Force, then spent five years in the Guard and a few more in the Army as a Signal Support System Specialist (25U2O). For his signal support role, he did have secret security clearance—but he'd never been involved in any secret ops. In fact, the only thing I recognized from Ty's paperwork was the note stating he'd been granted early medical retirement due to left-side paralysis. At least he wasn't lying about that.

After reading Ty's military file and all of his many accomplishments, I was baffled as to why he hadn't just told the truth about his real military career. He had plenty of commendable awards to be proud of and accolades of distinction that on their own would have earned him the admiration he desperately needed. However, Ty never mentioned any of the real awards during our four years together. As I continue to learn about the characteristics of narcissistic personality disorder, including the narcissist's tendency to embellish and exaggerate, I see Ty's lies more and more like icing on a cake. The foundation of Ty's cake was his position as a signal support specialist. To make his cake tastier, he iced it with seven combat missions, Colombian cartels, explosions and injuries, the taking of two human lives, and the burying of fellow soldiers in Arlington National Cemetery. In the end, his cake was all icing, so thick you could eat it with a spoon. There was no fluffy sponge, no substance requiring a fork. Instead of being proud of his genuine accomplishments, he chose to deceive and fabricate lies that would make him appear to be an American combat hero.

Role Reversal

The weekend after my attorney filed the petition for annulment at the county courthouse, Ty and I attended a financial seminar in San Antonio. I had booked this financial seminar prior to the discovery of Ty's parlor visits as an additional step to aid with marriage counseling. Determined to keep up my charade of ignorance, I insisted we go. The all-day seminar was emotionally and physically excruciating thanks to my severe tension headaches. Ty still knew nothing of the legal activity or private investigation happening in the background. How much longer was I going to have to pretend?

Knowing our marriage had an expiration date, I tested a hunch out of curiosity. I wanted to see how Ty would react if I told him my desire was to be at our Boerne home 100%, working remotely full-time with no more commuting back and forth to Austin. On a drive home one evening, I casually mentioned to Ty that I'd thought about it and I had decided to rent out the Austin house so I could be with him and the boys all the time. Ty's reaction told me all I needed to know. Before I'd even finished my sentence, he started talking over me. "What?!" he almost shouted. "You can't just spring something like that on me! I need to think about it. I'll sleep on it and let you know." Even though I was already on my way out of the marriage, his response confused and hurt me. What husband reacts to his wife with anger when she makes an effort to spend more time with him? Mine.

(Looking back, Ty's reaction was just more validation I was being used for supply. I was the only reason he and the boys had a home at all—in a resort community, no less. Ty had gotten what he wanted from me. Now that my supply was dwindling, I had become a nuisance.

Ty may have been operating under the idea that divorce, in Texas, results in a fifty-fifty division of community property, or all property purchased while a couple was married. But in the case of an annulment, there can be no community property since it's as if the marriage never occurred. Any titles or deeds therefore belong to the individual who purchased the property. Ty more than likely had a false sense of home ownership as, post-annulment, the house I'd purchased would be mine and mine alone.)

With the legal wheels in motion, it was time to break the news to my son. I knew he would take it hard; he loved Ty, too. I also knew I had to show him the proof in the pudding. After all, it's hard for anyone to digest the wrongdoings of someone they love. When the opportune time came, I sat at the kitchen table with my son beside me and I flipped through the financial data, the records of erotic spa transactions, and the documents proving a misrepresented military career. My son was very still and quiet as I turned each page. I was prepared for him to ask the question, "Are you sure, Mom?" Instead, he reached over to hug me, and we wept together. There was no question or doubt. In that moment, our roles as parent and child reversed. My adult son became my defender and protector.

Fraud Discovery #4 – Felony Jewelry Theft

Not long after I'd quietly filed the petition for annulment at the courthouse, I tracked my vehicle's GPS to the Boerne pawn shop. Ty had my car that day, and I watched as, for fifty-three minutes, it sat in the pawn shop parking lot. All I could think was, *I didn't even know Boerne had a pawn shop.* Then: *Why is Ty there?*

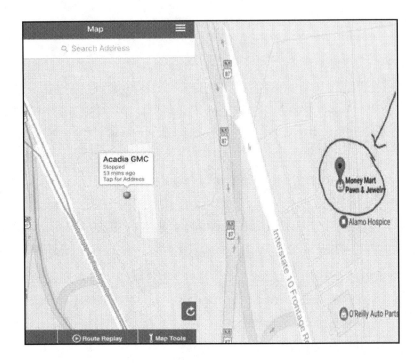

His stop didn't make any sense until I remembered the conversation with Sandy about my missing diamond ring. My heart sank and tears started to flow. She'd been right! I'd felt sure there was no way Ty would ever steal my personal property, much less property with sentimental value. But then again, I'd never believed he could have secret accounts, hidden mail, and frequent visits to an erotic massage parlor. After I regained my composure, I wrote an email and CC'd both my attorney and the private investigator. The investigator replied within seconds, saying he would get down to the pawn shop right away. I also sent Sandy a text message telling her where I'd tracked Ty to and she quickly replied, "I KNEW IT!!!" That's when I saw the GPS on my car begin to move. Ty was on his way to pick up my youngest stepson from school and then they would be coming home. I was a crying mess who had to get herself together fast.

When Ty walked in the house, I tried very hard to contain my emotions, but it was impossible. Ty could see I had been crying and he came over to find out what was wrong. All I could think to say was, "I've had a really bad work day and I was thinking about how much I miss my grandmother." My grandmother had passed away eight years prior. Ty knew we'd been very close and that I missed her every day. He hugged me tight to console me, unaware that what I was most sad about was having become a liar just like him.

I was desperate to get down to that pawn shop to see if my missing one-karat ring was in the display case. However, timing prevented me from doing so as Ty's mother was on her way over to stay the night with the boys. Ty and I were headed to Austin that evening because my friend Michelle was getting married the next day. Neither of us knew it at the time, but Michelle's wedding day would be the last meaningful moments Ty and I ever spent together as husband and wife. It was after her wedding—and after I confirmed my ring had been pawned—that I began my three-week evasion and absence from Boerne ... still pretending all the while, just pretending from a distance.

When we got back from Austin and I finally made it to the pawn shop, I circled the store three times without seeing my ring. Disappointed, I struck up a conversation with the store clerk, asking questions about the shop's process and how they ensured valuables were not stolen. She explained their policy was to hold jewelry in the back for thirty days to make sure no police reports were filed. Oh, good! As Ty had *just* been there the week before, my ring was probably in the back! I, like the private investigator, could not ask for more information without a subpoena, but my attorney was right then in the process of obtaining one. As casually as I'd entered, I made to leave, trusting we'd soon have the right to demand the ring—if it really was back there—be returned.

But then! On my way out, I felt a strong urge to take one more stroll around the display case. This is when I absolutely stopped in my tracks. My one-karat solitaire diamond ring was not in the case, but a smaller half-karat ring I didn't even know was missing was staring right back at me. I asked the clerk if she could take the ring out so I could look at it. After she removed the ring from the case, I took pictures of the tag and barcode. The ring was a size six. I was positive it was my ring! Still, I couldn't tell her it was mine or that it'd been stolen without first filing a police report. I walked out of the pawn shop with more sadness than satisfaction. My husband was not only a fraud, he was also a thief. Both rings combined were appraised at over $6,000. That's felony-level theft. The creatures kept coming out of the walls.

(After discovering Ty's jewelry theft, I thought about how ironic it was that Ty and I enjoyed watching Pawn Stars *on TV. We made a game out of trying to guess the outcome and the strategy of the bargaining. Unbeknownst to me, Ty was doing this in real life, with my valuables as well as valuables belonging to other family*

members. After the subpoena was issued and the PI engaged the pawn shop, he found records for many items that had belonged to other people in the family. The most disappointing find was that Ty had pawned his youngest son's camouflage shot gun, purchased for his birthday the year prior. Now when I think about watching Pawn Stars *with Ty, I feel as if he was privately mocking all of us given what he was doing in the background with our personal possessions. As for my rings: The PI got the smaller ring removed from the display case and placed on hold, but it turned out my one-karat ring had already been sold and was therefore unrecoverable.)*

My Secret Goodbye

As Ty's dark underbelly rose to the surface, I realized I didn't know my husband at all. *What causes a person to steal from his wife, children, and other family members?* I wondered. *What causes a person to lie for years about severe financial debt? What causes a person to frequent erotic massage parlors? What causes a person to misrepresent their career to family and friends? How distorted does a person have to be to do all of these things?* With the private investigation underway and gaining momentum, my heart scrambled for answers to these questions.

Secretly and in my own way, I began building up to my final goodbye. I started hugging the boys extra tight, knowing I wasn't returning and would, more than likely, never see them again. I told them more frequently how proud I was of them. I knew that eventually, in their eyes, I would be perceived as the enemy for exposing the truth about their dad. I gave Ty's mother a gift with a heartfelt note of gratitude as a silent goodbye. I took his sister to brunch and told her how much I appreciated her and her loving nature. I took Ty's oldest son to dinner one evening and focused purely on him and his bright future. I even walked room to room and said goodbye to the Boerne house that I'd bought for Ty and the boys. Ty frequently quoted an old English proverb: "Expect the best, but prepare for the worst." Because the annulment case could still go either way, I took his advice and walked away with the mindset that I had already lost everything.

My secret goodbye to Ty was much different. I had learned that I didn't even know who my husband really was. It was as if I was gearing up to say goodbye to a complete stranger with a familiar face. So, instead of thanking him, I used him for sex. Knowing it would be very difficult to ever trust another man again, I took from Ty the only thing he could offer me. The sex was emotionless and purely for my own physical satisfaction. Since I couldn't look at his face without feeling overwhelming sadness, I just closed my eyes. I used him like he was my prostitute.

We as humans are hardwired to believe in and protect the people we love. But sometimes, there's more than meets the eye—and that's when God helps us to see below the surface. Ty's wrongs were revealed to me, one after another, like a controlled burn. What appeared to me like a massive, out-of-control wildfire was really being divinely orchestrated. God was in full control of the flames as He put the right people in the right place at the right time. As I opened myself up to the Holy moments, God's grace found me in the midst of a mess, reminding me to trust Him and my instincts. What had been a natural instinct to protect my husband became pure instinct to protect myself. When something doesn't seem right, it might not be.

11

....

LIAR, LIAR,
WHEELCHAIR ON FIRE

"Truth cannot set you free until you know it."
—Pastor Buddy Owens

Weeks into the private investigation, I was fielding a lot of pressure from family and friends who now knew I was pursuing annulment and who were anxious for my attorney to just serve Ty already and get a court date scheduled. They all believed the investigative process was taking way too long. From their perspective, the attorney and the investigator had everything they needed to ensure a quick annulment (financial fraud, erotic parlor visits, stolen valor, and now jewelry theft). It was an open-and-shut case, they felt, with records to prove it. However, the voice deep inside of me told me to hold firm to the advice and recommendations of my legal team. The last thing they wanted to capture was surveillance of Ty visiting the erotic massage parlor in person. Even though the establishment's provider had been subpoenaed and the evidence was solid, my legal team insisted we wait for video footage, too. So, I continued to pretend like everything was "business as usual" with Ty.

To help catch him in the act, the private investigator asked me to turn the garage security camera to stealth mode. As this specific camera was mounted to the garage ceiling, Ty never unplugged this one like the interior cameras. In stealth mode, the blue LED light wouldn't be visible to Ty, so hopefully he'd think the camera was off. I, however, would still be alerted via a ten-second video of recorded movement, allowing us to track Ty potentially leaving for the massage parlor. I did as the investigator asked and turned the garage camera to stealth mode.

Fraud Discovery #5 – Walking!

The following day while at the corporate office, I received several alerts on my phone of movement in the garage. The video clips showed Ty taking the boys to school in the morning and then returning a short while later—nothing significant enough for me to prompt the PI. Later in the afternoon, around four p.m., I received another alert. It was time for Ty to go pick up the boys from school. Not thinking much about it, I watched the ten-second video. What I saw shook the very foundation of my reality and changed everything forever. It was the exact moment when I felt God saying to me, "Okay, Dee, this is what I have been waiting to show you. You've had enough. It's over."

(Ty walked perfectly across the garage floor!)

As I watched and rewatched this video, my brain almost shut down. I was so confused I could not process what I was seeing. Ty was walking perfectly! He had full function, shifting the full weight of his body between his good right leg and his paralyzed left leg, and his coordination was flawlessly balanced. His stride was confident and unencumbered. Ty was not hopping, scooting, or maneuvering on his right side. He was walking with ease and even switched a piece of paper from his left hand over to his right hand. Where had Ty's left-side paralysis gone?!?! I downloaded the video so I could keep rewatching it. Was I really seeing what I thought I was seeing, or were my eyes and mind playing tricks on me? If it was real, it would mean a lot of things I was not ready to accept. I was still trying to process the long list of Ty's other wrongs. Seeing him walk across the garage floor was too much for me to emotionally comprehend.

Before I forwarded this video to my attorney or the investigator, I needed a sanity check from a few of my loved ones. I sent the video clip to my son, Sandy, and Stephanie. The reaction was immediate and panicked. Sandy called me within minutes screaming at the top of her lungs, "HE'S FUCKING WALKING!" Stephanie texted me a few minutes later from a sales meeting and said,

"OMG, he's walking perfectly." Since I was at the office and knew I could no longer concentrate on work, I stepped into a team room and contacted my attorney. At that point, my little annulment case for domestic fraud became a full-blown federal fraud case with criminal intent. Ty was not only intentionally defrauding me, his wife, but he was intentionally defrauding the federal government. Further, it was clear that Ty's actions weren't just criminal, but sociopathic and possibly psychotic.

Ty got careless and walked for the security cameras again the following morning. This time, it wasn't just a short, ten-second video, either. The footage showed Ty walking with ease across the front porch, carrying our TV remote in his left hand while swinging both arms with full control. He straightened the cushions on our outdoor furniture with both arms and even stepped up on the front doorstep. He walked smoothly and with complete coordination on both his left and right sides. Just like the day before, there was no right-side hopping, scooting, or shuffling. As Ty stepped into the house to close the front door, he realized the security camera was on and recording. Unlike the garage camera, the front porch camera was not on stealth mode, and I watched him pull back the blinds to see the blue LED light. He knew he had made a mistake. Before he could erase the camera's history, I downloaded the video to my phone.

Exactly one minute later, I got another alert of movement on the front porch. This video showed Ty reenacting the same movements he'd previously made, straightening each cushion in turn. Except this time, he was hopping, shuffling, and scooting on his right side, his left arm dangling lifelessly as he dragged his limp left leg. This was how the boys and I saw Ty maneuvering around our home every day. The most profound moment of Ty's front-porch reenactment came when he was inches away from closing the front door. The audio very clearly and abruptly caught him saying to himself, "FUCK!" He knew his own negligence had just jeopardized two years of a dedicated handicap hoax. An Oscar for the brilliant conman posing as the perfect husband and an honorable disabled veteran!

Ty knew I was the only person who had access to the security alerts and the account. My theory for his back-to-back video reenactment was that he intended to delete the first one. Even if I had already seen it, he could delete it, and maybe the new one would convince me I was seeing things. Ty was very good at gaslighting me verbally, but this was his first and only attempt at video gaslighting. Same concept, different format. There was no way for Ty to know if he'd been caught without me saying something. What thoughts were running through his head as he realized his gig might be up? Probably, he was reassuring himself that even if I exposed his left-side lie, I didn't know about any of his other secrets. (So he thought.) My burden got a lot heavier and much, much scarier.

Seeing these videos of Ty walking perfectly gave me a feeling of euphoria and devastation all rolled into one. For two years, I'd thought my husband was disabled and had no function on his left side. I had been cutting his food, for goodness sake! What kind of human being can do this to another human being, especially their spouse and children? My family and friends, meanwhile, felt more panic than devastation. If Ty was capable of faking a disability for over two years, they worried, of what else might he be capable? After all, he had everything to lose and nothing to gain. It didn't matter that Ty had never, not once in four years, exhibited an ounce of physical aggression. (If anything, he was always cool as a cucumber—too cool—even during heated conversations. At times, I wished he would have shown some type of emotion during disagreements that warranted a little anger!) My son, Sandy, and Stephanie were adamant that I stay in Austin and not go back to the Boerne house. They all strongly believed that if Ty found out I'd seen the videos, I'd be in danger. I listened to their advice.

Most Shameful of All

With the walking videos in hand, there was no longer any reason for the investigator to capture surveillance of Ty visiting the erotic massage parlor. In the grand scheme of things, my petition for annulment had become insignificant compared to what now constituted a federal case. As new documents were drawn up to serve Ty, I stayed in Austin but talked to him on the phone like normal. Since I never mentioned the security camera footage, I think Ty believed he was off the hook. My husband knew me well. If something bothered me or didn't seem right, I would vocalize my concern immediately or ask a million questions without hesitation. Given my non-reaction, he must have thought his secret was still safe. Well, it was not.

In between me seeing the initial walking videos and Ty being served with the annulment papers, our security cameras captured more than twenty additional videos proving Ty's left side was fully functional. The most heartbreaking one showed Ty using his left arm to pick up one of the boy's heavy backpacks. He gripped it with his left hand, bent his left elbow, and lifted it up high using his left shoulder. Out of all the videos captured, this was the only one that made me break down and cry, because it meant Ty could have hugged his boys with both arms all along. He could have thrown the football with ease. He could have cast a fishing rod. He could have swum in the pool.[1] Instead, he chose to deceive his kids. While I had a lot of breaking points along the way, this video is what finally cracked my heart in two. It was crushing, surpassing even the heartbreak of the erotic massage parlors. Ty paying for full-service sex was a travesty against me, his wife. But Ty pretending not to have full use of both arms was a travesty against the boys, his chil-

---

1   Three weeks prior to the discovery of the initial garage video, Ty and I had attended Easter church service and gone to lunch at my brother's house. On this day, no one including my family knew that I was in full-force "pretend mode," just like I didn't yet know that Ty was faking his paralysis. At church, Ty utilized the handicap parking spot, the handicap ramp, and the ADA wheelchair seating area in the sanctuary. When we joined my family for lunch, Ty hopped on his right side to maneuver around my brother's house. As usual, I filled his plate with food for him then cut his Easter ham. After lunch we all went out to the back deck and watched the kids play in the pool. Ty seemed a little down, so when we left, I asked what was bothering him. He told me it made him very sad watching our nieces and nephew play in the pool because he used to be able to do the same with his boys. His confession also made me very sad. Before he was paralyzed, I had enjoyed watching him toss the boys around the pool while throwing his waterproof watch so they could search for it underwater. Anymore, thinking about this conversation only makes me mad. Ty could have played in the pool with his boys, but he consciously decided to forego activities with his own children for the benefit of fraudulent financial gain.

dren. This is absolutely the most shameful of all.

With hindsight being 20/20, I will always wonder what else might have been discovered if those garage cameras had been turned on stealth mode earlier. Some of the videos show other people in the garage with Ty, or offer snippets of one-way conversation as Ty talked to unknown others on the phone. The visitors were never people I recognized. They came one at a time and typically carried clipboards or briefcases. My best guess is still that these individuals were the contractors and inspectors involved in the bid and approval process for Ty's $80,000 VA home-adaptability grant.

My addiction to Ty's love bombing was so strong that even during my early discoveries and throughout the private investigation, I continued to second-guess myself. I wondered if the financial fraud, prostitution, and jewelry theft was something I could just buckle down and plow through to keep my marriage intact. I loved Ty. However, all my second guesses evaporated when I saw him walk across the garage floor. There was no amount of narcissistic intoxication that could make me overlook the sociopathic behavior staring me in the face.

Served

While the official investigation continued in the background, my son, Stephanie, and Sandy formed a trio of amateur detectives. They became their own investigative team, sharing research, information, and updates. As I tried to maintain a full-time job in the corporate world and pretend to have a normal marriage with Ty, my trio were following hunches and developing conspiracy theories on their own. Stephanie even took it upon herself to house all the duplicate photos and videos, becoming my "eye in the sky" and redundant data center lest something should "happen" to me. At the same time, my parents were doing their best to support me from afar. Fully "in the know" now, too, they found it hard to stay put in their small Texas panhandle town and not run to my rescue, though they understood doing so was important for keeping up appearances. It helped knowing that, for almost the whole time I had to maintain normalcy, my support system was in place and stronger than it had ever been.

My son was with me the day Ty got served. I couldn't see nor hear my husband's reaction, having already blocked his (and sadly, the boys') numbers at the advice of my attorney. The document Ty received was a generic Petition to Annul Marriage. It listed no specifics other than "Respondent induced Petitioner to enter into marriage by fraud." The hope was that Ty would assume I'd filed for annulment based on domestic fraud alone. The legal team didn't want him to know I knew everything until our day in court. Included in the paperwork was a Protective Order with a temporary restraining order that mandated all communications go through my attorney. From this moment on, I had zero contact with Ty, the boys, or his family.

Unfortunately, the two younger boys were home when Ty was served. I was hoping to avoid this, but the timing was critical. It had to be that evening in order to expedite our court date; otherwise, we would have had to wait over a month due to scheduling. The next day, Ty removed the garage camera from the ceiling and disabled it. He covered the security camera on the front porch with black electrical tape, probably not realizing the audio was still functioning. I was able to hear, though not identify, guests to our home without the visual. This was important because Ty had been warned that *anyone* visiting the property other than himself or the boys, even his mother, would be considered trespassing. Yet Ty continued to have strangers at our house.

Summary of Benefits

As there was a high probability that a federal fraud investigation was imminent, I was asked to assemble a summary (to the best of my knowledge) of all the organizations from which Ty had received benefits. I thought this would be an easy task since as far as I knew, Ty received monthly disability deposits from just two departments: the Veterans Administration and the Social Security Administration. These benefits had been coming in a steady stream for almost two years and totaled roughly $6,800 per month in tax-free funding. Well, it wasn't that easy. The investigators wanted a list of every organization from which Ty had received "resources"—not just money. It could have been physical items or services provided by the government, for-profit, and/or nonprofit organizations. Since Ty's first medical claim upon his return from Germany, he'd received disability resources from at least nine different people or organizations that I could recall. These included the Wounded Warrior Project, the Fisher House Foundation, Resources for Reservists, Operation First Response, the Semper Fi Americas Fund, the Warrior Family Support Center (WFSC), VA Vocational Rehabilitation, Wish for our Heroes, and several private citizens in San Antonio and the surrounding areas.

As I totaled up their in-kind goods and services, everything from gift certificates for fuel and food to tickets to professional sports games, I estimated Ty had been given the equivalent of $280,000 in free gifts. That number included the $20,000 VA vehicle grant Ty had recently used to purchase a new 2017 Dodge Journey, but not the $80,000+ housing grant he was still in the process of obtaining to remodel and retrofit our home with handicap accommodations and new appliances. This housing grant, also awarded by the VA, would be placed on hold after the judge who heard our annulment case ordered Ty to vacate the Boerne property. The amount of funding Ty had received from various organizations was shocking. After adding it all up, I couldn't understand why he was always short on funds as the end of each month approached. Where was all this money going?

(The list of organizations that provided Ty with disability benefits is quantifiable. What Ty took from disabled Americans and deserving veterans, on the other hand, is not—though it's equally immoral. Ty spent hundreds of hours in therapy, undergoing medical testing, and attending doctor's appointments. Every one of these hours Ty stole from other veterans needing critical healthcare. It's not easy getting accommodating appointment times at the medical centers. Some veterans have to wait for weeks or even months to

see specialists. Not only did Ty consume these VA resources, but while onsite, he utilized handicapped parking spots and took pride in being a fellow Wounded Warrior, when in actuality he was far from it. The suicide rate for veterans today is alarming and growing, but Ty didn't flinch at taking their psychotherapy spots. There are wheelchair-bound vets who dream of standing tall with honor, yet Ty chose to use a wheelchair when he could really walk. His actions were reprehensible, disgraceful, and immoral.)

On a local level, there were also individuals and organizations that assisted us during the transition to our new normal after we left the comforting arms of the Fisher House. A local ministry and men's group from the Curry Creek Baptist Church rallied a group of people on New Year's Day to help us move from a third-floor to a first-floor apartment that was wheelchair accessible. These individuals took time away from their families on a holiday to help us. On that day, I was deeply humbled by their generosity, but knowing what I know now, I feel ashamed. Other community organizations like Veterans Services, Angels all Around You, and other home-grown businesses offered Ty free goods (tanks of gas, gift certificates) or services (auto repairs, legal advice). All of these people and organizations were victims of Ty's fraud.

Divine Intervention

The private investigator was the first person to give a name to Ty's classic narcissistic traits. Before he did, I thought a narcissist was just someone who was arrogant and admired their own appearance. If I had only known the telltale signs of narcissism and how this disorder aligns with sociopathic behavior, maybe I could have saved myself earlier.

Narcissists create drama and manipulate their environment for personal gain as well as sport. It seems extraordinary that Ty spent more time and energy working to be a conman than it would have taken for him to get a real job and be a real man. Instead, he chose to be a fake man—to lie, steal, manipulate, and hop around on one leg. It must have been absolutely exhausting, not to mention deleterious. Ty's right leg only hurt because he chose to hop around on it as the default leg. The aching joint pain in his right hip and knee were the result of purposeful overcompensation to avoid using his left side. All his own game.

I say I could have saved myself earlier, but I didn't save myself, not really. During my journey, the Holy Spirit was like my GPS. My steps were guided by profound clues. The clues were abundant and came crashing down like a ton of bricks at precisely the right time. When I had no strength left for the fight, the Holy Spirit gave me the power and the people to keep moving in the direction God was pointing me. This was no random coincidence. It was the presence of God. God called for evidence to fall into place. There's no way all of the puzzle pieces would have fit without God having His hand in it. It was divine intervention. I'm convinced of it. His timing is perfect.

12

....

THE SURFACE

"Nobody can be kinder than the narcissist while you react to life on his terms." —Elizabeth Bowen

Narcissists are skillful at ingratiation. They use abundant kindness to influence and manipulate, and will bend over backward seemingly to please others when really, it's all about social control. Ingratiation allows them to seduce both their own community and their victim's support network friends, family, neighbors, and co-workers—to establish social control. Think about it: A person who has no enemies has power over everyone. That control, while empowering to the narcissist, often leaves their victim feeling isolated and alone. Even more so when the victim is the only one who sees the person standing behind the curtain.

Ty's Community

Boerne, Texas is a picturesque little town in the Texas Hill Country that has all the warmth and wholesomeness of a Norman Rockwell painting. To walk Main Street is to stroll into a past era, carried by the smell of bakeries, breweries, and locally owned BBQ and burger joints. The streets are lined with pedestrians shopping at specialty boutiques and antique shops. The weekends always pull the surrounding communities for farmers' markets or vintage car shows. During the holidays, there are the usual festivals, plus memorials for soldiers past and present at Veterans Park. Every spring brings county rodeos, while football season brings parades. The Cibolo Creek rolls through the center of downtown and its banks are the perfect spot for family picnics, fishing, and feeding the ducks. This Hill Country town is the epitome of American nostalgia.

Ty was a king in Boerne. His irresistible charisma made him intoxicating, inviting, and appealing. He always looked people directly in the eye, engaging and acknowledging everyone. When he reached out to shake hands, he would typically pull that person in for an enthusiastic hug and a strong pat on the back. He greeted acquaintances with terms of endearment such as buddy, chief, sweetheart, honey, and darling. You could bet on him starting most conversations with, "Let me ask you a question"—an attentive gesture that made the other party feel important, especially when Ty then tried way too hard to emulate that person's interests as if they were his own. Indeed, everything Ty did was designed to make people feel special, which in turn won for him their admiration. Like a politician canvassing for a vote, Ty needed that approval. Only, Ty wasn't on any ballot for an election.

Early on in our relationship, Ty used these methods, as well as the adulation of his community, to win my admiration, too. On many occasions, men and women came up to me to tell me how lucky I was to be with Ty. Men would say, "Ty is a great guy" or "He would give the shirt off his back to anyone." Women would whisper, "I'm so jealous" or "He's so handsome." Even the boys' pediatrician told me once at a football game, "Ty is a great dad to his boys." In essence, the community of Boerne, Texas helped sell Ty to me. They made me more confident that, yes, I had found the perfect man. And on the surface, Ty is precisely what they say. They couldn't be more correct about what they observe from the outside. However, the man underneath would be unrecognizable to them. Even as I write these words, I have a hard time digesting the reality of the man who lives beneath the surface.

After his many years in Boerne, Ty had accumulated hundreds of acquaintances. But, he had very few significant relationships with people who were emotionally invested in his day-to-day life. He had a handful of close friends, but even these he kept at a distance unless he needed something from them (a tow, a ride, legal advice, or another favor). Many times, I asked Ty to invite his friends over for dinner or drinks, but they would always have a schedule conflict or last-minute emergency. In my four years with

Ty, we only extended one successful social invitation, and this was before we were married, never afterward. We rarely went to social events ourselves, either, and if we did, it was for a brief appearance with very little time to socialize. On the other hand, we never missed one single sporting event for the boys. Theirs were the only guaranteed activities with opportunity for free-flowing social interaction. Even then, Ty or his mother would point out people in the stadium who were friends of his ex-wife, making me hesitant to engage anyone for fear of where their loyalties lay.

Being an outsider in Ty's community was hard. Most everyone in Boerne knew about Ty's and his ex-wife's turbulent divorce, and even though it had happened before my time, it somehow became part of my history, too. The ladies in the community were kind to me overall, though I sensed an element of resistance to fully embracing me as a friend. By and large, they were friends of Ty's ex-wife, so as much as I would have enjoyed real friendships with them, I knew our interactions would be forever limited to the superficial. This was convenient for Ty, as it meant that in the end, I could just vanish with no residual impact to him, almost as if I'd never existed. However, the residents of Boerne still knew I was a good person. Whenever our paths did cross, they hugged me warmly and I felt their genuine care. I will always be grateful for the consideration they showed me during my time in that small town.

Those who knew the real Ty have compared him to Ferris Bueller, the main character in the popular 1980s movie *Ferris Bueller's Day Off*. On the surface, Ferris is charismatic, popular, and seems to be an all-around great guy. He appears to be working toward everyone else's best interests, but in reality, he is a cunning master of deceit. Behind the scenes, he lies and toys with people's emotions and resources in order to get what he ultimately desires. He's so skilled at the craft of manipulation, cloaked in slippery charm, that people don't even notice they're being used. In the end, Ferris comes off as the community-wide hero while the people who supported him are destroyed. Like Ferris Bueller, Ty consumed those closest to him for his own supply and to their detriment. Although he, too, was a "community-wide hero," a disabled vet deserving of sympathy, Ty's story ended much differently. Ty's truth has been exposed.

My Community

Like the good people of Boerne, my social network was suckered by Ty's charm, too. My son, parents, friends, neighbors, co-workers, and even my boss all grew to love him, and he became an integral part of our lives. Everyone took Ty at face value for the great guy he appeared to be. They couldn't see that just as he was mirroring me, he was also mirroring the likes and dislikes of my loved ones, fashioning himself into everyone's best buddy.

It was after my adult son met Ty, spent some quality time with him, and said, "Ty's the kind of man we all hope to be when we grow up" that I was sold on Ty as a partner. It seemed a very profound statement from the mouth of my own child, whose thumbs up I needed more than anyone else's. Ty treated my son as if he had known him all his life and always greeted him with a warm, affectionate embrace, just like he did my parents. My mom especially was a big fan of his tight hugs, and the fact that he called her "Mom" when she visited. My dad was intrigued by Ty's military background and could talk to him easily for hours. Ty always showed interest in my parents' farming and ranching business, which is a point of pride for our whole family. He also asked questions about their individual family histories and listened with rapt attention to their childhood recollections of events as they were growing up. My brother and his family also loved Ty. My nieces and nephew adored their Uncle Ty.

It was no surprise, then, that Ty made a positive first impression on my closest friends as well. Two friends did warn me that "If he seems too good to be true, maybe he is," while another flat-out told me, "He tries way too hard." At the time, I ignored these comments, though considering what good judges of character they are, I should have paid closer attention to them. As time passed, Ty began randomly calling or texting my friend Sandy in the Texas panhandle. He would reach out to her just to ask how her day was going—a move I found odd and somewhat intrusive. The first time he called her, she thought there was an emergency because it's not normal for your friend's boyfriend (or husband) to call you out of the blue for a long chat. All I can say is that love makes it easy to overlook the warning signs.

On several occasions, Ty invited my boss to have drinks. This made me uncomfortable as I felt it compromised the professional relationship I had established with him. In all my years working for him, I'd never had drinks with my boss, but that didn't stop Ty. Ty also began texting my boss occasionally (just like Sandy). I asked him to please stop—my job was my livelihood and I felt Ty was making things awkward. Ty was upset by my request, but I thought it was a fair ask. If he'd had a job, I'm certain he wouldn't have wanted me to text his boss, either.

All of these people—family, friends, everyone—felt betrayed and saddened when our annulment went through and the unbelievable things Ty had done became common knowledge. I was not Ty's only victim. My support system and social network were also victims of Ty's narcissistic criminal behavior. He inflicted widespread hurt on all of us. We loved him. We trusted him. And, we believed him. We invited him into our lives, only to be held hostage by his twisted truth, since we all had to keep the fact of his fraud secret as the federal investigation was underway. In this sense, I didn't grieve alone; we all grieved together.

God knows who you need and when you need them, and He puts them in your life at exactly the right time. My family and friends ran to my rescue the moment they heard about the magnitude of Ty's deceit. In my childhood home, a plaque hung on the wall that read *Faith will guide you, family will believe in you, and friends will hold onto you.* I always loved that notion, and in my case, it's been proven true. Look for God in the people close to you. He's always with us. Once I opened my heart and shared my despair, God made His presence known with a cascade of divine signs that poured down like rain. Our job as human beings is to carry one another. My family and friends carried me through the most difficult time in my life. When one soul touches another, there is a ripple effect. Every challenge is a spiritual opportunity for not only the receiver but the giver.

My newlywed friend Michelle once told me a story she'd read about wildlife scientists in the African desert observing herds of elephants. The herd will instinctually rally to rescue a vulnerable elephant in distress by protecting it from predators. They encircle the defenseless elephant until it's able to stand and manage on its own. The elephant herd serves as a force field, a ring of protection, an impenetrable wall. Their circle displays the pure unity of unconditional love. My support network became elephants. They rushed to protect me like a herd of African elephants, taking time off work, missing meetings and family events, driving and flying hundreds of miles to surround me in a ring of protection. They stood tall when I could not, sheltering me through the layers of discovery, the months of pretending, the annulment process, and the very long wait through the federal fraud investigation. I have endless gratitude for all of my elephants.

13

FEED THE FISH

"Sometimes, you just have to play the role of a fool to fool the fool who thinks they are fooling you." —Shu Takumi

The day of the annulment hearing was a day I will never forget. It had been an interminable five weeks since I'd discovered Ty could walk, and two weeks since he'd been served with the annulment papers. All I could do was hope and pray the outcome would be in my favor. Overwhelming even my anxiety about our court appearance was a sadness that pervaded my whole being. I felt as if I was getting ready for a funeral rather than a legal proceeding. Regardless of how the judge ruled, it would still be the day I said goodbye to the man I loved. As I dressed and got ready, I prayed to God to make me emotionless and stoic during the hearing. The last thing I wanted to do was show my deep sorrow in front of Ty, the attorneys, and the judge. God answered my prayers and made me a robot. I took strength from knowing I wasn't being weak and bailing out on my marriage; I was being a person of integrity by fighting for myself and the truth.

The night before the hearing, I stayed with Stephanie since she lived in the area. We woke up, had coffee, got ready, and left her house with enough time to accommodate potential traffic delays. My other friends, who were also witnesses, had already arrived in Boerne the night before and were staying at a hotel not far from the courthouse along with my son and my parents. My brother drove from Austin to the courthouse that morning and we all met in the foyer thirty minutes prior to the scheduled hearing at nine o'clock.

It was a beautiful morning, sunny and warm. But for the life of me, I don't remember the drive. My mind was clouded by a million scenarios of how the day could unfold. While I sat in rush-hour morning traffic, Stephanie following in her car behind me, I received a text from my son, the most precious gift he could have given me. His timing was perfect. It simply read, "It will be a good day, Mom. I love you."

As Stephanie and I entered the courthouse, we were greeted by my brother and the private investigator in the hallway. They had both been there for a while but didn't know each other. I introduced them. Then my protector, my son, arrived. He was my strength and never left my side the entire day. Everyone started filtering into the courtroom and it was time to start.

While we were stuck trying to get comfortable on the hard wooden benches, my parents went to the Boerne house to lock everything up. If things didn't go my way and the judge ruled in Ty's favor, I wanted to make sure Ty wouldn't try to take what wasn't his. First, they placed a steering wheel lock on my secondary car, the one Ty had been using. Then, they set up camp inside the house and waited for the rest of my family and friends to show up. Our "group plan" was for everyone to be there when Ty returned, hoping it would make him so uncomfortable he would leave the property. My support system was in place. But … where was Ty? And where was Ty's attorney?

Five minutes past nine, there was still no sign of Ty. Finally, we learned he was in the courthouse parking lot, sitting in his brand-new car and occupying the handicapped spot. He'd purchased the car only two weeks earlier using the $20,000 VA vehicle grant, then had proceeded to tell others in the family that he'd paid cash at the dealership. The car had been bought with cash, just not his. The American people paid cash for it.

After Ty got out of the car and wheeled himself into the building, it became clear that he and his attorney were unprepared for court. The district judge appeared frustrated by their lack of respect for either the justice system or the scheduled start time, giving me some extra points right off the bat. To my surprise and great relief, upon conferring with his attorney, Ty agreed to proceed with the hearing. That meant the evidence—all of it—could be shown in court. Ty had no idea what had been discovered nor what bombshells were coming his way. It's likely he still thought I was pursuing annulment due to financial fraud, the original reason we'd started marriage counseling. But I was ready to confront him about the massage parlor, the jewelry theft, the stolen valor, his misrepresented military history, and the biggest con of all … his disability fraud! Our side enjoyed a brief moment of excitement knowing Ty was about to be called out in front of the district judge and the courtroom attendees. It was all I had wanted for months, and that victory alone made my otherwise unbearable task of "conning a con" worth it.

It was communicated to my attorney that Ty wished to proceed with the hearing because he wanted possession of the Boerne house. Well, of course he did. I'd set him up in a beautiful home in a golf resort community. Not only had I bought it, but I'd also furnished it. Because Ty had made mortgage payments with his VA and SSA disability funds, he thought he had a right to the house. To my logical mind, you have to pay to live somewhere and provide for your children. No one lives for free. Ty must have forgotten about the tens of thousands of dollars I funded upfront at closing to get him, my disabled husband, and his boys out of an apartment and into a one-level home that would accommodate a severe handicap. With that, the hearing started.

The Hearing

Everyone settled into their seats, including the witnesses. The massage parlor owner and "provider" had been subpoenaed and was sitting a few rows behind me. The pawn shop manager had also been subpoenaed and was present. My family and friends sat directly behind me. My son, my brother, the private investigator, and my attorney sat to either side of me. On my side of the courtroom, a crowd filled every available seat, while across the aisle, only Ty and his attorney formed a tiny army. Where were his mother, his support system? Had he even told them about the hearing? It didn't seem so, since the seats on his side of the courtroom remained completely empty.

My attorney and her two legal assistants were prepared for a long day in court with their laptops queued, several stacks of documents at hand, the hard evidence and walking videos ready to present. Ty's attorney didn't even have a pen or a piece of paper. This is when I started feeling sorry for Ty. What I saw across the aisle was my helpless "surface husband." In a moment of empathy, I forgot about the reality of the man underneath. Ty found a spot across the room to fixate on and he didn't take his eyes off of that spot during the entire hearing. He barely blinked. Like me, he, too, was an emotionless robot, one that sat perfectly still as if unplugged.

Once each attorney had made their opening remarks, the judge ordered them both into his chambers, where my attorney presented our evidence to the judge and opposing counsel. Opposing counsel was seeing the data for the first time and was taken by surprise, so much so that he was pissed! He could only be mad at himself, though, since he had not bothered to call my attorney prior to the hearing for any information or pre-wire. As for my side, we were thrilled. Opposing counsel's reaction confirmed we'd done a good job of keeping everything concealed. Ty's secret self was finally exposed—just behind closed doors instead of in the courtroom, where I'd hoped Ty would be faced with his own reality.

Ty's attorney left the judge's chamber and abruptly ordered Ty to follow him out of the courtroom. I watched Ty try to maneuver in his wheelchair through the low, swinging double doors. Seeing him struggle made me flinch. My instinct, as always, was to get up and help him, same as I had for the past two years. It didn't matter that Ty was pretending in a room full of people who knew he was faking. I was, and still am to a degree, in denial that the person I loved was using me for financial gain. I sat on my hands and crossed my legs so I wouldn't run to him.

After a little time had passed, my attorney called me out of the courtroom and into the legal library across the hall. She looked at me with a very serious face and said, "Okay, he's really, really scared now." Ty had been made aware that his lies and deceit were floating on the surface for everyone to see. Even so, when we all met back in the courtroom for the final ruling, Ty stayed sitting in his wheelchair, persisting in a charade that had been fully and publicly debunked. It was surreal—though maybe not as surreal as what happened next. Standing before the judge's bench, myself and my attorney on the left, Ty's attorney on the right, the judge ordered Ty in no uncertain terms to vacate the property at once. He had twenty-four hours to pack his and the boys' belongings and be gone. Like that song says, Ty didn't have to go home, but he couldn't stay there.

One Condition

Ty caved to the ruling on one condition. He wanted me to agree not to discuss the details of my annulment petition with anyone else or to pursue state or federal criminal charges against him for fraud. I agreed readily, knowing his efforts to keep the annulment details under wraps were in vain. Authorities had already begun the process of pursuing federal charges. Even if I never said another word, Ty would be served with litigation on the basis of everything I'd previously shared. What mattered to me was that I'd been freed from a fraudulent marriage based on lies, deceit, and manipulation. My attorney had gotten me out of a fake marriage to a fake man with a fake disability. I would never be hurt by Ty again.

There was a flurry of activity as my attorney composed a quick handwritten annulment decree. I sat there numb, knowing I should feel liberated but completely unable to breathe. I desperately needed a moment alone so I could have the meltdown that had been building for months. After the attorneys went to the bench and the judge signed the annulment, I asked my counsel if I could address Ty directly. All communication to this point had gone through our attorneys, and I was unsure if I was allowed to talk to him because of the Temporary Restraining Order against him. My attorney said yes, but advised me to wait until everyone had left the courtroom before I approached Ty.

Out in the hallway, I stepped aside and waited for Ty to exit. It seemed as though he was lingering inside, perhaps waiting for everyone else to leave. Finally, he wheeled out into the hallway.

With my son and my brother beside me, I stepped in front of his wheelchair and said, "Ty, you need to tell the boys you are fully functional. You've been able to hug them with two arms all along. They deserve to know that." Ty looked me straight in the eyes and promised he would. Those were his last words to me. And they were, in themselves, an admission of guilt.

(Ty never did come clean to the boys. It was their mother who told them their dad was a fraud and could really walk. The only piece of information she withheld from them was Ty's patronage of the erotic massage parlor. That was something they didn't need to know, she felt, and I agreed.)

The Aftermath

After the hearing, everyone went their separate ways and back to their normal lives. Sandy went back to the hotel and waited for me to wrap everything up with my attorney. I held it together all day and was the robot I'd prayed to be until I drove to the hotel where Sandy and her husband were waiting for me. The moment I saw her face, it was as if a walnut had cracked open and I was finally able to let my emotions flow. She held me tightly in the corridor while I wept uncontrollably. I was free. Free from years of deceit and narcissistic manipulation, free from being married to the man I still loved. Legalities and court hearings were now over for me, though they were just beginning for Ty.

Sandy, my son, and my parents stayed through the following

week to help me complete the Boerne house transition. We all avoided the house during the twenty-four hours Ty had to collect his things, but once that window had closed, Sandy accompanied me to the place I'd once shared with a man and his sons and never would again. As the garage door went up, I was surprised to see that Ty's belongings in the garage were untouched. Very little inside the house had been boxed or moved, either. It was as if he'd packed an overnight bag for a weekend getaway, like he thought he was coming back. The dishwasher in the kitchen had just been turned on and was still running. The shower was still warm with a wet towel thrown over the door. Ty had even left a note on the kitchen counter on a torn piece of typing paper, asking me to "feed the fish." I was speechless. Then I discovered the one thing Ty had been sure to take: the entire "pharmacy" from the second shelf of the master bathroom closet. Some things, I realized, never change.

With Sandy's help, I hired movers to come pack all of Ty's and the boys' things and put them in a storage unit. I included everything I'd bought and furnished for the boys. We gave the keys to the storage unit to Ty's attorney, who was under strict instructions not to hand the keys off to Ty until he'd reimbursed me for the packing, moving, and storage unit rental. A few weeks later, Ty wrote me a check and it actually cleared. To this day, I don't know where he got the $3,000 to repay me, but at last, we were square.

Sandy took care of everything else I wasn't emotionally capable of taking care of on my own. She remained calm and a pillar of strength as she organized my parents, security companies, locksmiths, real estate agents, movers, and storage facilities. She became my "boots on the ground." Just like I wouldn't have survived pre-annulment activities without Stephanie being my "eye in the sky," I wouldn't have survived the immediate post-annulment period without Sandy, my son, and my parents. My elephants had once again surrounded me.

When the fog began to clear, I was overwhelmed with feelings of gratitude for my family and friends. They held me up when I didn't have an ounce of hope left.

14

....

MORE CREATURES
IN THE WALLS

"You don't have to be strong to survive a bad situation; you simply need a plan." —Shannon L. Alder

Narcissists will always have an excuse or an elaborate explanation for their bad behavior. They are never accountable. A narcissist will offer differing variations of what happened until the receiver either accepts one of the versions, or they become so exhausted with the whole conversation that they just give up. Narcissists' words rarely match their actions and they will always deny any wrongdoing. Don't hold your breath waiting for them to accept fault because they have a praiseworthy sense of entitlement that leads them to believe their behavior should never be questioned.

Rather than admit they are the perpetrator, they twist events or conversations to make themselves appear to be the victim.

Excuses

A few days prior to our annulment hearing in late May, Ty "predicted" the miraculous end of his paralysis. He mentioned over lunch with a family member that he was having a medical procedure in June that would restore his ability to walk. Ty was already walking, of course, but at the time he thought he was the only person who knew it. This mysterious procedure, which he refused to describe with any level of detail, was nothing more than Ty's excuse to begin walking again. He was greasing the skids for a plausible story that the boys would easily accept. Needless to say, Ty did not have a procedure in June that "made him walk." His prearranged cure became obsolete as soon as my legal team exposed his fraud. If he didn't know it before, Ty learned very quickly during the annulment hearing that all medical records can be subpoenaed. Womp-womp.

When Ty was made aware that the boys had seen the videos of him walking with full functionality on his left side, he did his best to explain away how this had happened. He told the boys he had taken a new drug that had made him black out. This drug, he said, must have allowed him to walk, though he had no memory of doing so. What was this wonder drug, you ask? Funny, I asked the same thing. You'd think if Ty was truly convinced in his own mind that a drug had made him walk, he'd be so excited he would have shared the news immediately with his wife and doctors. But no. Ty had to be confronted with video evidence before the farfetched story came to mind.

It was a story Ty stuck by for a long time, adding to it as needed. For example, the spontaneous memory loss soon started occurring when he was driving as well. He would show up somewhere unable to remember how he'd gotten there. Interestingly, these lapses only afflicted him when he was alone. He never walked or blacked out when anyone else was around or in public places. A primary trait on the Factitious Disorder checklist is *only exhibiting symptoms while in the presence of others.* Ty was only paralyzed when he knew other people could see him. Alone, he let his guard down, and the security camera saw him.

Every child on the planet wants desperately to believe their parent is telling the truth. It's reprehensible that Ty used positive mirroring to deceive his own children. He knows they are devoted to him and they want to believe every word that comes out of his mouth. Even though his story didn't make any sense, they swallowed the Kool-Aid and moved on. I can only imagine what kind of psychological impact Ty's lies have made on his sons, boys who deserved better, who deserved the truth.

For months after the annulment, Ty lived without penalty or consequence for his criminal conduct. Sure, he'd lost me, his wife, but he'd otherwise "gotten away with" domestic fraud. He still had joint custody of the boys and continued to receive regular, large sums of tax-free money from the government. As far as he and the strangers he passed in public were concerned, Ty remained an honorable disabled combat veteran, not an ounce of remorse or guilt to his name. Ty was living the narcissist's dream, but it wouldn't last long. The feds were just around the corner!

Post-Annulment Mockery

Several weeks post-annulment, Ty and I both received a group text from a friend we'd met during our extended stay at the Fisher House. Our friend was retiring with military honors and asked that we attend his ceremony at the Warrior and Family Service Center (WFSC) located on Fort Sam Houston. Neither Ty nor I replied to the group text. The retiree had no knowledge of our annulment, and rather than awkwardly try to explain it, both Ty and I stayed silent, no return text.

I was on the fence about attending the party. I wanted to go to support our friend and his wife, who are both amazing people, but I didn't want to see Ty there. Over the next week, I convinced myself Ty wouldn't have the guts to show his face. It would just be too unscrupulous, even for him. The honoree had lost the use of his legs when they were crushed between a building and an out-of-control vehicle during a military training exercise. Not only is he in a wheelchair, but he lives in constant pain. He's always attending therapy or undergoing another surgery. Our friend is a true American hero. His wife, too. If Ty showed up to the ceremony in his wheelchair still pretending to be paralyzed, he'd be mocking a "real" honorable disabled veteran.

Fast forward to the retirement party ... I chose not to go. Ty did attend. And, he arrived in his wheelchair as a paralyzed veteran and wounded warrior. It is absolutely disgusting and obscene that he attended this celebration while still pretending to be disabled. Especially since numerous people and elected officials from Boerne knew of Ty's fabricated aliment. That Ty dared to mock our friend in this way is borderline, if not full-blown, psychotic. Shame on him.

Fraud Discovery #6 – Falsified Legal Documents

It shouldn't have been possible, but post-annulment, more hidden creatures started coming out of the walls. Documents surfaced on an old laptop that Ty and I had shared for a short while. This laptop was sitting on a shelf in my office when I remembered Ty had used it for a few months during the spring. Out of curiosity, I pulled it down. Ty had wiped it fairly clean but there were a few eye-opening documents still hibernating in the recycle bin and downloads folder. I should have looked at this laptop earlier, but what I found wouldn't have affected the end result of our annulment proceedings. However, it did enlighten me as to the implausible extent of Ty's premeditation and planning. There were documents in the Photoshop application that had absolutely no business being there. Turns out, Ty was also an expert at Photoshopping legal and official documents.

Among my discoveries: Ty had falsified the dates on his previous divorce decree. This is how he was able to cover up four years of lies about being divorced when we met. It's truly beyond my heart's understanding that I did not know Ty was still married for eight months while we were dating. To learn this after our annulment was another devastating blow. If I would have known this fact when we met, I never would have dated him. My moral compass would not have allowed it. Still, when I discovered this Photoshopped divorce decree, many events I'd been told about during our first year together made a lot more sense. I'd had no reason to question Ty back then because he'd given me a physical legal document with dates that matched his story. It was more heartbreaking proof that I had been living a lie from the very beginning.

More lightbulbs went off when I found his 2015 personal bank statements and the sales receipt for a vehicle purchase. Again, both had been Photoshopped to cover up lies he didn't want me to discover. Ty had removed his ex-wife's name from the top of their 2015 personal bank statements because the account had been joint, not individual, and he didn't want me to know. The sales receipt proved he'd purchased the vehicle with his mother. She had co-signed the loan to offset Ty's poor credit. I had asked Ty for both documents when preparing our first joint tax return as a married couple. Oh, I got them. But, they were the versions of the documents he'd falsified in Photoshop.

The only ones I never figured out were Ty's military annual performance reviews, which I also found doctored copies of on that laptop. As I couldn't restore the originals, I still wonder what he changed on those documents and why. Obviously there was something or he wouldn't have gone to the effort. It's a curiosity I may never have the answer to.

Meanwhile, in the downloads folder, I found some telling residual documents that Ty had failed to delete. The VA guidelines for Special Monthly Compensation Ratings Form 3.350-1, for example—a form used to determine disability compensation—had been extracted from a larger file. Ty hadn't downloaded the entire file, just the disability compensation part. It seriously looked like a study guide. As I read through it, I saw that Ty had claimed every single disability ailment on that extracted document. No wonder he'd been able to obtain a 170% disability rating from the VA (100% loss of use of one hand and one foot, 30% migraine, 10% tinnitus, 10% impairment of sphincter control, 10% neuralgia of the fifth cranial nerve, and 10% impairment of field of vision). He'd studied how to work the system for each specific ailment on the document. The more ailments you have, the more disability money you get. Toward the end of our marriage, Ty had complained of urinary and bowel incontinence, one of the ailments listed on the extract. Even though Ty had expressed concern about incontinence and had attended several VA doctors' appointments for the issue, he had never purchased any adult diapers at the store. Nor had he requested any. Later on during the federal investigation, I was asked by a special agent if Ty had ever peed or pooped the bed, or wet himself during the day. My answer was no. I should have heeded this alarm bell when Ty first mentioned his incontinence, realizing there was never any physical evidence.

A few documents were interesting but not as intriguing as the others, including several letters from the Army Incapacitation Review Board (IRB) denying Ty's claims for incapacitation pay and a letter from his Primary Care Manager (PCM) at Brook Army Medical Center listing his recommendations for Ty's treatment. These had been downloaded but not moved into Photoshop, so there was no indication of foul play like with the others.

Discovering these falsified legal documents and additional untruths were just more surprises lurking in the dark. I believed there couldn't be any more wrongs to be found. But, I was naïve. There were so many strands comprising Ty's web of lies. I'm sure there are more secrets still waiting to be discovered.

Even as I was finding these old falsehoods in documented form, I was also watching Ty blaze a new path of destruction from a distance … for now, he had a new victim.

15

....

RINSE AND REPEAT

"A normal person can't just turn love off—but a narcissist can turn it off just as easily as they turned it on because showing love is a tool they use to con people." —Author Unknown

From everything I've learned about narcissism, I now believe I was Ty's tool from the very moment we met. After all, he was still married when we began dating, and then he started visiting the erotic massage parlor before and during our marriage. If I had any outstanding doubts, they were quashed the day I heard, only a few short weeks after our annulment hearing, that Ty had a new girlfriend. His behavior fit a common narcissistic pattern. A narcissist can move on easily without a care in the world. Literally.

No matter how earth-shattering the trail of devastation they leave behind, they remain indifferent and remorseless. When a narcissist feels backed into a corner, they scramble, panic, and typically begin looking for a new source of supply even before the old source is gone. They create a brand-new sense of reality and project an illusion of happiness. Just like Ty had with me upon his first marriage ending, after our marriage ended, he quickly found a new target with an abundant source of supply and no distractions. His pattern began again. Rinse and repeat.

From the outside, it seemed Ty had moved on at lightning speed. It was shocking to me that he could so easily turn love off and on like a light switch. Within weeks, he was sweeping another victim off her feet, which is classic narcissistic behavior. My natural instinct was to run as fast as I could to warn his new victim. But, I could not risk tipping Ty off that he was under federal surveillance. He had to continue his day-to-day activities as usual while the special agents worked the steps of their investigation. That left Ty free to catch a new victim in his spider's web of deceit, and left me feeling helpless to save her.

I knew exactly how it was playing out, too. At his most sinister, Ty comes across like a baby bird with a broken wing. He seems innocent and lovable, which makes women want to take care of him. But Ty plays with emotions like they are a magic trick up his sleeve. He uses the love bombing and the mirroring to lure unsuspecting victims, and by the time they've taken a bite of his juicy red apple, it is too late. They've already been poisoned. Convinced they are soulmates destined to be together from the day they were born,

Ty's victims feel both proud and undeserving that Ty has chosen them as a lifelong companion. When he says, "I've been searching for you my whole life," they swoon, thrilled to be the one saving Ty from complete and total despair. After all, he is handicapped *and* the casualty of two failed marriages—marriages he did everything humanly possible to save. Ty has always been the martyr, has always made all the sacrifices. He is the victim, not his romantic partners!

Watching Ty's narcissistic cycle continue was torture to me. At least in his new relationship, he didn't have to lie about being single; we truly were annulled. I'd served him the papers, I'd stood in front of a judge in a courtroom, and I'd said goodbye to marriage knowing that I still loved him. But who I loved was the Ty on the surface, the Ty mirage, not the Ty who took everything from me (financially, emotionally, and physically) only to drop me once he'd exhausted my supply. Things were different for his new target in that respect, too. She didn't have to spend years working to get Ty back on solid financial ground or endure his constant medical trauma. I'd already done all of that. No, what she got was a different Ty mirage, the polished product of his insidious efforts and my downfall. Her Ty arrived unshackled by fake paralysis hurdles, unnecessary medical appointments, bogus therapies, and ridiculous schedule shuffling. I still wouldn't have wished him on her or anyone else. No matter who Ty traps like a bug in silk, their "fairytale romance" will always be cemented in a foundation of lies and deceit.

I no longer lose sleep over what Ty did to me. But, I do lose

sleep knowing Ty's sons continue to suffer as involuntary participants in his intentional fraud and that Ty will never stop drawing
in new victims. I can't forewarn or protect them all, but maybe I
can help you, dear reader. Then something good will have come
from all this pain.

Prince Charming Is a Predator

Even after we were no longer married, Ty's credit alerts continued to come my way. I'd previously had myself added to all of
his reports so I could help him rebuild his credit to a decent standing. All it took was making him pay his bills consistently and by the
due date. Post-annulment, his improved credit scores quickly fell
back into the poor category. He applied for and was denied several
personal loans and credit cards. His existing accounts went into
default again, then many of them went to collection. There was no
reason for this since until the federal investigation concluded, Ty
was still receiving an absurd amount of tax-free money from the
government each month. Where in the world did all that money
go?!?! I could only hope he hadn't roped his new victim into paying
his way like I did.

(*The same week the government authorities informed Ty he was
under federal investigation for fraud, they also met with his new
victim and presented her with the evidence. She was made aware
of Ty's severe federal fraud as well as told the details surrounding my annulment case. After I heard the truth had finally been*

passed onto her, it made my heart much lighter. A considerable amount of my inner turmoil had stemmed from not being able to protect her from the lie she was starting to live and the inevitable storm that was brewing on the horizon. I prayed that she would accept the truth and protect herself. She is not unique for having fallen for the seductive claws of this specific narcissist. Prince Charming is a predator.)

16

....

ALL SQUARED AWAY

"God sees that justice is done." —Proverbs 2:8

My hope that justice would be served didn't come from vengeance or anger; it came from wanting to do the right thing. In the end, it was about truth and morality. Deserving civilians and disabled military veterans all over the country are even now being taken advantage of by crafty criminals like Ty cheating the system. There are working, yet financially strapped, vets who live paycheck to paycheck to make ends meet, homeless vets living on the streets, and vets with unaddressed mental health issues. At time of writing, an average of 16.8 vets per day commit suicide, making suicide the second-leading cause of death behind accidents in that population.[1] Above all, there are struggling Gold Star families whose brave husbands and wives, sons and daughters, laid down their lives and made the ultimate sacrifice for our country. Meanwhile, Ty made it his job for years to work the system and execute fraud with his phony disability.

But the real tragedy is that Ty's trickery went much deeper than government fraud. My hope for justice, then, was also about doing the right thing by his boys. They didn't deserve the life they were forced to live, knowing their dad was intentionally simulating a disability for sympathetic attention and financial gain. Ty emotionally manipulated them by using their unconditional love for him as a tool, making them the worst victims of all. I was able to walk away with hope of rebuilding, but they will never be able to walk away. Most parents sacrifice for their children. Yet, he sacrificed the well-being of his boys for his own sociopathic needs. What Ty has done to his own children is utterly beyond criminal.

Most would think that standing up for truth is easy. But, when children will ultimately be impacted by the downfall of their father, it's an excruciatingly painful decision. Nevertheless, the choice was clear. I chose truth, morality, and the goodness of God. I understand and accept that in the eyes of Ty's boys, I will always be the enemy. That's okay. There was a reason my perfect marriage began to fall apart. Someone had to stop Ty. Someone had to do the right thing.

---

1   "National Veteran Suicide Prevention Annual Report." Office of Mental Health and Suicide Prevention. September 2022.

The Investigation

Shortly after the annulment case closed and a select set of elected officials and other professionals in Boerne, Texas were made aware of Ty's fraud, they took action. A federal investigation involving agents from both the VA and the SSA was underway within the month, though it would take five long years before we saw any kind of resolution.

During the investigation, several of my "elephants" were interviewed as witnesses. These family members and friends were happy to follow protocol and play by the agents' rules, whom we all agreed were sharp and impressive. Federal agents in general have tenured backgrounds in criminal behavior and fraud and know how to navigate the federal justice system. With dozens of years of experience under their belts, they don't waste time or resources on a case with no chance of making it to the floor of the U.S. court system. They only extend resources when there is strong evidence of real criminal conduct—and in Ty's case, there was. He may have been a fake man, but he was a real criminal.

As investigators overlaid the timeline I'd supplied with the timeline they'd reconstructed, Ty's fraud looked more and more like a house of cards stacked several layers high and about to collapse. They uncovered disability claims I knew nothing about—claims Ty had filed before we were married stating he needed assistance with the activities of daily living even then. Moreover, by comparing claims submitted to the VA and the SSA, they saw where Ty had provided conflicting information to these agencies—enough to have caused the VA to flag Ty's file as "suspicious" all on their own (something I was told happens very rarely). The special agents validated everything I had come to believe toward the end of our marriage and then some. Some information they shared made me feel better, while other tidbits and facts made me feel worse. "No offense to you," one agent said, "but he's a highly intelligent criminal, very calculated and strategic." No offense, was he kidding? Hearing that comment was actually a big relief! It meant I'd been the victim of a highly intelligent conman and wasn't just a stupid or naïve person. On the other hand, the comment "It's rare to see disability fraud where other family members are not involved" made me cringe until I learned I was *not* a co-suspect. They suspected certain other family members, but were never able to prove it.

It was also these investigators who introduced terms like "narcissist" into the mix. According to them, and as my research corroborated, a narcissist will do anything not to be discovered. Public exposure of his crimes would therefore, they thought, be a more effective deterrent for Ty than prison time. Certainly Ty had proven he was both interested in and capable of constructing false identities in order to win admiration. He seemed to believe these constructed selves were infallible and invincible—and to be sure, he'd wiggled his way out of so many lies. Eventually, though, the game had to end. Ty would face the consequences of the United States justice system, and I would face the (continued) consequences of having fallen in love with a narcissist.

I accepted that I was the outsider exposing Ty's fraud to an entire community. Revealing Ty's secret self to the good and decent people of that Hill Country town was hard for me to swallow, but necessary. They truly believed he was the pure definition of an American soldier and honorable veteran. School-aged children recognized Ty as a military hero and were in awe of his perceived Army career. I was ripping the mask off of their Batman. But I had to, to limit the number of future Ty casualties. The more people who know who he really is—or at least how to recognize a narcissist—the better off the world will be.

The Opposite of a Lie

Waiting for notification from the U.S. justice system that Ty had been served gave me extreme anxiety. The tension headaches I'd been suffering from were now accompanied by cold sweats and panic attacks. All I could do was take deep breaths every morning and trust in God's plan, knowing that everything happens on God's timing, not mine.

I also distracted myself with research into Narcissistic Personality Disorder and Factitious Disorder, wondering the whole time what had happened to Ty to make him like this. Something profoundly tragic or emotionally impactful must be deeply seated in his past. Something is suffocating him, and his fabrications are helping him breathe. Did he learn by example? Was it a predatory animal instinct? Will I ever know? Does he even know? Ty's lying goes beyond habit. There's something itching underneath, like an addiction. According to the *Harvard Business Review*, shame drives compulsive behavior and chronic lying is an addiction driven by fear.[2] If fear is Ty's motivation for lying …what is he afraid of? What void is Ty trying to fill?

Throughout the investigation, I was the one who had to lie. Once, I was unaware of the sinister activity taking place beneath Ty's magnificent surface. Later, he was unaware of the secret surveillance and mounting case being built brick by brick behind the scenes. While I was having panic attacks, he was in the eye of the storm, where the winds were calm and the air was peaceful. But the inevitable storm was swirling all around him, and it was the opposite of a lie. It was called "the truth."

Federal Investigation and Surveillance

The local Boerne VA Service Officer was the first to push the red button that lit a fire under Ty's federal case. The fraud claims submitted against Ty may have sat in a pile of thousands of other claims for who knows long had this man not elbowed them to the front of the line by using his VA network connections. Unfortunately, the service officer had to continue to help Ty even though he knew Ty was a fraud. Every time Ty wheeled into his office asking for assistance and government benefits, this man had to smile and play along. Just like my play-acting at the end of our marriage, the service officer's pretending must have been equally difficult. He knew the "real" Ty, and I thank him personally for his

---

2   Chamorro-Premuzic, Tomas. "How and Why We Lie at Work." *Harvard Business Review*. 2 January 2015.

valiant service to our country.

He was not, however, the only person pushing the red buttons. My friend Stephanie filed two fraud claims, one with the VA and the other with the SSA. That's how adamant she was that Ty not "get away with" his dirty deeds and that nothing fell through the cracks. She didn't trust the government bureaucracy so she took it upon herself to make sure claims got filed. The VA Office of Inspector General (OIG) was the first to schedule an interview with her. Her interview lasted several hours, during which time she provided a detailed overview of the events leading up to my domestic case for fraud and an explanation of how the walking videos had been discovered. Since Stephanie had been my redundant data center, she was able to take copies of all of the falsified legal documents, transactions, pictures, and videos with her to the interview. She had first-hand knowledge of every detail, having been beside me from the very beginning.

When I was contacted by the agents for my interview, the phone call was bittersweet. Even though I wanted to expose the truth, my heart still loved the person who lived on the surface. It had been explained to me early in the federal investigation that communication regarding the case would be mostly one-way (in the special agent's direction). But, if they could answer my questions, they promised, they would. I provided them with all of the information they requested and was contacted several times for follow-up data, videos, and pictures. In return, they shared what information they could, which confirmed I'd not been wrong or wildly off-track. Each time, our conversations were quick and to the point, no messing around. I've never been so impressed yet so intimidated at the same time.

On one call, the federal agents mentioned Ty's was one of the most severe cases of fraud they'd seen in their dozens of years of investigation. Even though they'd seen monetary fraud of much greater value, Ty, they said, had "one of the worst M.O.'s" (modus operandi) they'd encountered. While no formal criminal personality profile was ever compiled on Ty, a few psych experts not directly involved in the case commented in passing that Ty's narcissistic behavior was abominable, suggesting he fit the profile of a malignant narcissist. My own research led me to believe that Ty more accurately fit the profile of a covert narcissist—but that distinction's not what mattered. What mattered was that a professional in the field had confirmed Ty was a narcissist, assuaging some more of the guilt and horror I was feeling about having been conned by him.

In an effort to come to terms with being married to a narcissist posing as an honorable disabled vet, I asked one special agent if the military doctors thought Ty had always been faking the disability or if any of it had been real. There's a part of me that would like to believe not all of my life with Ty was a lie. The answer, however, was what I expected. Professional opinions from several military doctors pointed to Ty's paralysis being fabricated from the very beginning. Two separate neurologists had noted "doubts" during Ty's follow-up visits to their offices, including the Traumatic Brain Injury specialist who'd recommended Ty seek psychotherapy. My former husband had a condition, all right—it just wasn't paralysis.

Brand-New Affliction

Ty was made aware that he was under federal investigation exactly one year to the day the first walking video had been captured. On that one-year anniversary, he was brought in for an interview with both the VA and SSA federal agents. The coincidence felt like God was giving me yet another wink, a further reminder to trust in His perfect timing. I hoped Ty would come clean that day, that as soon as he knew he'd been caught, he would give up. The interview that was scheduled to last a few hours, however, took almost five hours, extending right into the middle of the afternoon. "He's a talker," one agent said during a break. Didn't I know it.

I found out later that Ty's response was basically to plead the fifth. He didn't seem to recall walking or being fully functional—ever. His explanation was that he'd taken a mixture of drugs that might have made him ambulate, but he didn't remember. (This was also when he said he couldn't remember walking down the aisle at our wedding, crushing my spirit.) When the agents asked if he wanted to see the videos of him walking, Ty refused. Oh well. They already knew who he was and what he had done. (It's possible the government knows Ty better than he knows himself.) A confession would have been nice, but it wasn't crucial. He'd been investigated from top to bottom and inside out. They'd watched his patterns and isolated his lies. After the interview, one agent commented on Ty's arrogance, marveling at how Ty had really seemed to believe he'd fooled a room full of professionals. "Ty thought he was the smartest guy in the room," another added. If he had been, he would have known what he was up against.

The day after Ty's initial interview with the SSA and VA federal agents, he was hospitalized following what appeared to be a seizure. Someone at the place where Ty now worked in IT had found him unconscious in an equipment room and called 911. The medical staff noted symptoms of epilepsy, but there were no abnormalities on either his MRI, EEG, or EKG. I wasn't surprised. This brand-new ailment fit his pattern of inducing drama as a distraction tactic. Like the goose egg on his forehead from the bathroom drawer, it was yet another example of malingering with a side of Factitious Disorder. Dueling personality disorders competed for the limelight as his theatrical performance continued. Ty had fallen back on his most reliable tool in an attempt to escape the truth with trauma and sympathy. And why not? At that point it still had a 100% success rate. Sadly for Ty, the episode did not stop his VA and SSA disability benefits from being suspended or keep Ty from being charged by the U.S. Attorney's Office with five counts of federal fraud.

Ty's newfound affliction of seizures—which he'd never suffered from prior to being confronted by federal agents—continued on and off for a while. Sometimes they resulted in the by-now-familiar head contusions.[3] Always, these injuries occurred when no one else was around to witness the inciting accident, and always, they occurred in visible places on his body, never underneath clothing where they couldn't be seen. One incident in an apartment com-

---

3   A 2015 article by Steven Brian Nimmo in medical journal *Occupational Medicine* states that 39% of "illness deception" cases involve minor head injury. Ty's pattern is not unique, but a tactic used by others who fabricate illnesses.

plex parking lot was so "severe" that EMS, police, and firefighters were all called to the scene. Ty was discharged from the hospital after the ER physician who examined him said it was "impossible" Ty was seizing—his pupils weren't dilated and further, he seemed to have conscious control as his arm was raised and dropped from above his forehead. Ty's arm should have fallen naturally across his face but instead it fell to the side. Another time, Ty began seizing at a follow-up doctor's appointment. The family member with him insisted Ty be taken to North Central Baptist Hospital in San Antonio, not the Boerne ER (where, presumably, they knew Ty was full of it). The ambulance took him to the Boerne ER, though, where doctors could find nothing wrong with him. Was all of this Ty's attempt to build a fraud-defense-by-seizure?

Shortly after the North Central Baptist Hospital fiasco, Ty glommed onto something called Functional Neurologic Disorder (FND). FND is a neurological disorder causing weakness, movement disorders, sensory symptoms, and blackouts where the brain appears normal but functions incorrectly. Instead of telling the truth and owning up to his years of financial deception and federal disability fraud, Ty tried frantically to find a doctor who would give him an FND diagnosis before he got summoned by the U.S. court system. If he had FND, he would have an alibi for his behavior, setting the stage for a last-ditch not-guilty plea.

The checklist for Factitious Disorder includes ailments that morph over time as personal circumstances change. The individual's exaggerated symptoms may mimic illnesses or injury, have no root cause, get worse for no apparent reason, and/or be sustaining.

They may make frequent trips to the ER, endure extended hospital stays, and/or seek care from multiple medical facilities, all in an effort to con their families, doctors, or other relevant parties. Did Ty have Narcissistic Personality Disorder, Factitious Disorder, or both? His symptoms were neck-and-neck and too close to call.

Narcissists will never admit they are at fault. They refuse to believe they've done or said anything wrong. They will not reason; even if deep down inside they know the truth. They will lie, twist the argument, blame others, or invent elaborate excuses to keep the truth from rising to the top. Narcissists always maintain a sense of superiority over who they talk to or deal with in a given situation. This characteristic holds true for Ty. He believed he could outsmart his physicians, convincing them something was physically wrong with him when his test results kept proving otherwise. When Ty made the conscience decision to fake paralysis, he alone changed his fate forever.

(After Ty's family found out about the active federal investigation, one of his family members made a threatening statement. They had two bullets, they said, and one was meant for me. This family member described in detail how they would plead senile, go to jail, and enjoy three meals a day and free healthcare. Hearing this made me uneasy and sad. I loved Ty's entire family and was good to them while we were married. Yes, my exit was extremely abrupt, and I left with zero explanation. I'm sure the animosity ran deep with their inadequate understanding of the events. If they only knew the real reason I'd quickly escaped, then

threatening statements of ending my life with a bullet would not have been so forthright.)

Speedbumps

I have faith in the system. And, my faith is two-fold. I have first-hand experience with how government agencies such as the SSA and the VA do indeed take care of civilians and military members with medical challenges. I've seen the quality of their services, the kindness of their staff, and the generosity of their financial assistance with my own eyes. Secondly, I've seen that justice will be served to those who abuse it. Criminals who steal from the American people and honorable veterans will be stopped. It may entail a lengthy investigative and legal process, but the system does work.

As I waited for confirmation from the federal agents that Ty's case was proceeding, I was made aware of a speedbump in the case. The yearlong investigation was complete and in the hands of the U.S. Attorney's Office. However, the prosecutor working Ty's case had suddenly retired and the agents had to wait for the case to be reassigned to a new U.S. Attorney. It's as if both the VA and SSA federal agents had successfully driven the ball to the goal line but the officials had thrown a flag and called an unexpected timeout. This timeout lasted almost four months.

Then, there was a secondary speedbump. After the case had been reassigned to a new U.S. Attorney, the federal government shut down for the longest duration in the history of our nation (thirty-five days) due to political turmoil in the Trump administration. Many jobs within the federal justice system were furloughed and their offices shut down. While the government closure dragged on, federal cases continued to pile up with no movement or staff to work them. The case backlog grew.

No one ever could have anticipated the third speedbump, coronavirus! Due to the COVID-19 worldwide pandemic, most of the American workforce came to a screeching halt and was homebound. The federal court system was no different. Once again, federal cases began piling up, creating a backlog that would take months or possibly years to sort through.

These delays initially pushed Ty's case from an anticipated summer completion to the following spring. Ultimately, it languished several years longer than anyone had expected due to multiple resource constraints, two unexpected government shutdowns, and a global pandemic. It seems the only thing that didn't cause a delay in his case was an alien invasion from outer space!

Through it all, the federal agents working Ty's case remained more than gracious when it came to answering questions, providing updates, and treating me with the utmost respect. It wasn't their job to make me personally feel better about being a victim of domestic fraud or to put me at ease regarding the slow federal investigative process. But, they always tried. The VA special agent in charge spent dozens of hours talking with me over the duration of almost five long years. Not because he had to, but simply because he was a good person. He could have easily blown me off. But, he didn't. Even though communicating with federal agents was extremely intimidating, the VA special agent always made me feel like my questions were just as important to him as they were to me. He gave me hope that the truth would win. His confidence kept me strong throughout the process. On some days, all that kept me going was knowing I was right—and the federal agents' belief that I was right, too.

Somewhere along the friction-filled path of multiple U.S. Attorney's Office delays, Ty's case was recategorized from criminal to civil. This had its pros and cons. Pro: Criminal charges have to be proven beyond a reasonable doubt, while civil charges do not; so, it would be easier, theoretically, to get to a conclusion. Con: If found liable, Ty would not be classified as a felon; he had to be convicted of criminal charges to earn that title. I wanted Ty to be classified as a felon. He was a criminal. He'd committed so many crimes! But, I also understood the court's reasoning. First, Ty had no previous criminal history. Never had he been considered a danger to himself or others. His crime was financial, not violent. Pretending to be paralyzed didn't endanger society. Second, according to the agents, the outcome of the case was likely to be the same either way. Whether convicted as a criminal or liable as a civil offender, Ty was unlikely to get jail time. The best-case scenario we could hope for, they said, was that Ty would be ordered to repay all of the money he had stolen, times three. A civil case, meanwhile, would consume fewer resources than a criminal case. It was basically a "Let's take the road less bumpy" approach.

There is still a part of me that wishes they would have pursued criminal charges. After all, there is a local legal precedent. In 2017, Mack Cole, Jr. of San Antonio was sentenced to federal prison for twenty-seven months for defrauding the VA.[4] And that was just the VA! Ty defrauded *two* government agencies. Why was the U.S. Attorney so quick to assume that Ty would get off without jail time?

Federal Fraud Charges and Settlement

While the U.S. Attorney's Office was wrapping up Ty's case, Ty began walking in public with no wheelchair in sight. He must have sprinkled a little pixie dust, cured himself, and ditched the wheelchair. There was no logical transition from a wheelchair to a walker to a cane. He went directly from the wheelchair to walking. It was a miracle! I guess since Ty hadn't heard one peep from the federal special agents during the months and months of multiple delays, he assumed he'd gotten away with his fraud, no repercussions. At that point, why would he continue rolling around in a wheelchair if he was no longer getting an absurd amount of free government benefits? So, he miraculously cured himself, having no idea that the hammer of justice would imminently fall. Ty set himself up to "walk" right into a summons for federal fraud.

In May of 2020, exactly three years, one month, and three days after Ty walked across our garage floor on video (not that I was counting or anything …), the U.S. Attorney for the Western Dis-

---

4   "San Antonio Man Sentenced to Federal Prison for Scheme to Defraud the Veterans Affairs Disability Compensation Program." United States Attorney's Office, Western District of Texas. 21 September 2017. https://www.justice.gov/usao-wdtx/pr/san-antonio-man-sentenced-federal-prison-scheme-defraud-veterans-affairs-disability

trict of Texas officially filed a civil lawsuit against Ty. He was personally served by a U.S. Marshal and the VA special agent in charge with a summons that included five counts of federal fraud against the United States of America (plaintiff). My short abbreviation of the counts below:

1. First Cause of Action - False Claims Act, 31 U.S.C. 3729 (a)(1)(B). False record or statement to receive compensation that would otherwise be denied. The United States government asked for three times the damages they suffered, totaling $598,190.13.

2. Second Cause of Action – False Claims Act, 31 U.S.C. 3729 (a)(1)(G). Knowingly making false record, statements, omissions, or concealing information. The United States government asked for three times the damages they suffered, totaling $598,190.13.

3. Third Cause of Action – Payment of Mistake Fact. Obtaining funds that were not properly payable. Payments made on the assertion of disability were issued by mistake of fact, for which the United States government was entitled to recover $199,396.71.

4. Fourth Cause of Action – Unjust Enrichment. Obtaining federal funds to which one is not entitled. Damages determined at trial.

5. Fifth Cause of Action – Conversion of government property. Obtaining funds that belong to the United States and acting with malice. Damages determined at trial.

In addition, Ty would be held responsible for attorneys' fees, court costs, and other expenses incurred by the United States government.

Ty did everything he could to prolong and drag out the inevitable by filing with the court system two Motions to Extend and four Motions to Stay over a two-year timeframe. In the end, he did exactly what everyone had expected. He settled out of court to avoid a humiliating trial that he could not win. The federal fraud case was officially closed and dismissed in May 2022—almost five years from the beginning of the federal investigation in August 2017.

The tide had turned. Instead of the government paying Ty for a fake disability, Ty had to reimburse the federal government for everything he'd purposefully taken, plus restitution. As of today, Ty is still paying the consequences of stealing from American citizens and honorable disabled veterans. Hats off to the VA and SSA federal agents for bringing justice to the people. I had hoped for criminal charges and jail time, but I am comforted by the fact that at least he was caught and is facing the music. The long, excruciating wait for justice was finally over. Closure.

17

....

LET IT GO

"Sometimes God redeems your story by surrounding you with people who need to hear your past, so it doesn't become their future." —John Acuff

What's the recipe for forgiveness? What's the recipe for recovery? I thought I would find the ingredients somewhere inside my obsessive search for information on Narcissistic Personality Disorder and Factitious Disorder. The secret sauce doesn't lie in education alone, though, and I'm realizing the path to recovery doesn't taste the same for each person. And unfortunately, it's not an overnight fix. The journey back to myself after full narcissistic consumption is a slow and ongoing process of self-healing and restoration. I long to be the person I was before I met Ty. I find myself looking for glimmers of hope that she still exists. I went from an unsuspecting, head-over-heels target to an empathetic victim to a ripped-up survivor. Now my struggle is not just learning how to endure, but learning how to fully live again. I'm trying not to grieve over something I cannot change. I also realize I cannot run from what happened to me; I have to integrate it. Although that part of my story is over, I still have to work, consciously, toward moving forward and letting go.

For years, I built my world around a man who pretended to be many things he was not. My marriage to Ty wasn't a fairytale after all; it was a nightmare. I had a front-row seat to a four-year theatrical performance and didn't know I was an involuntary participant in his hand-picked cast of players. Realizing this, and understanding that I had been living a fabricated life from the moment Ty and I met at the Austin diner, left me emotionally devastated—some days seemingly beyond full repair. My truth was purposefully altered by the person I loved. Mourning the loss of Ty is profoundly difficult because I have deep sorrow over someone who never really existed. The real Ty was a delusional sociopath pulling the strings of my puppet show from behind a velvet curtain.

After the chaos subsided, words could not describe the pain and betrayal. I didn't know how to talk about what I'd been through, so I didn't. Group engagements felt like forced obligations as I went through the motions. I dreaded family and social responsibilities where I had to put a smile on my face and pretend to be normal while inwardly I was suffering. This in itself seemed like a form of fraud, and further contributed to the debilitating thoughts that were like pollution contaminating my days and sleepless nights.

Another side effect of narcissistic abuse is that after your eyes have been opened to it, you begin analyzing everyone around you. You become paranoid. I suddenly saw narcissistic traits in many of the people I'd engaged over the years (acquaintances, co-workers, family members). I became leery of interactions with new acquaintances and no longer tolerated any person or situation who made my spidey senses tingle. I literally exited conversations mid-speech if I felt those patterns were present. As a result, silence and isolation became my safe spaces. I retreated into the quietness to heal myself, knowing my absence would not be judged by the people who truly loved me.

The word forgiveness is very complex. God tells us to forgive our neighbors as He has forgiven us. I can say that I've forgiven Ty and even convince myself I believe it. But, the strong desire for justice and truth still occasionally creep in and take over. When I think about his lack of remorse or apology (we have not interacted directly since the annulment hearing), my heart has a difficult time stitching up the last little bits of forgiveness that I should bestow upon him as a Christian woman. Especially since I must remember, narcissists do not have the capacity or ability to feel remorse. Narcissism is a behavioral illness.

For that reason, as I make a mental list of every inhuman wrong Ty has committed, I have to look at my own list. I remind myself that everyone has a dark side. No one is flawless. And, I'm far from shame-free. I've made more than my fair share of bad decisions over the years—decisions I still regret. I was not only a victim, but I was also an enabler of the worst kind. I naïvely believed Ty even though my intuition was constantly nagging me, screaming at me that something was out of balance. I swept the blaring signs under the rug and ignored the spiritual taps on my shoulder while stumbling all over myself to ensure my disabled husband got everything he needed for himself and his boys. I allowed my former husband to fully manipulate, consume, and control me. Because of this, he used my own goodness against me. The scariest thing about Ty was that he wasn't scary. I trusted him more than I trusted myself. I must take responsibility for those deeds. Like Ty, I have also caused pain and betrayed others who cared about me. Given my own personal baggage, it should be easy for me to pull the door shut and forgive. So, that's what I pray for every day now: to truly forgive Ty, whom I loved before he broke me. And, to forgive myself for not knowing what I didn't know. I pray that both Ty and I will be defenseless against my prayers. After all, Ty, too, is a child of God.

My counselor, whom I continued to see long after the case was closed, once told me, "Ty is not the enemy." As soon as I heard those words, I agreed. His behavior was the result of his illness. It was Ty's narcissism, not Ty himself, that hurt the people around him. If I had only listened to my inner voice earlier, I may have been able to vaccinate myself against the ruthless virus called narcissism. Because I didn't, because I couldn't, I'm doing what I can do now: sharing my story so you can get your "shot."

What I've Learned

In the end, my agonizing experiences have also been richly meaningful. They have taught me, for example, not to judge people because all of us are suffering. Everyone is going through something distressing that they shove deep down inside. Every soul walking this earth has pain old or new, big or small. Love is the key to humanity and kindness is the engine that turns the wheels. The smallest gesture of kindness, like a smile, a hug, or a compliment, could be the lifeline that keeps someone functional for a moment as they struggle to put one foot in front of the other. When my grief was at its peak, a store clerk told me I had a "kind and beautiful smile." It was a small comment, but meaningful enough to keep me afloat on a day I felt sure I was sinking. I still think about that person today and how their compliment made me pivot from despair back to neutrality. It reminds me to be much, much kinder to everyone I encounter. There are individuals who don't just struggle to live day by day; they struggle moment by moment. Don't let the opportunity for kindness slip away. What may seem minor to the giver could be a powerful, lifesaving act of compassion for the receiver.

My experiences have also taught me to pay more attention—specifically to people who decrease my energy. To anyone noticing hints of potential narcissism in their relationships, I urge you to observe carefully, ask questions, and test your theories or suspicions to see what reaction you get. If the outcome fits the checklist of narcissistic traits, proceed with caution. When there's an instinct burning inside that you cannot explain, interrogate it. Listen to your inner voice because it comes from a spiritual and divine place. If the nagging voice gets louder, do not ignore it. Your soul is telling you something is very wrong, and your body is picking up the bad vibrations. Your conscience is always in your corner and your gut instinct protects you from danger. This organic alarm bell is the signature of God on your soul. It may be hard breaking free from the enslaving love bombing and seem illogical to throw away a relationship that appears to be what dreams are made of. But, that may be all it is … a dream and pure illusion.

Victims of narcissists often form biochemical bonds with their abusers similar to those that can develop between an addict and their drug of choice. Making the decision to detach from a narcissist can emulate drug withdrawal because the brain's chemistry has relied for so long on the release of oxytocin (the "love hormone" that promotes attachment and creates co-dependency). There is also a phenomenon known as trauma bonding. This occurs in a victim when their abuser's reward and punishment tactics entangle them too deeply for them to let go. Essentially, the victim stays loyal to the person who is destroying them. But, staying in a relationship with a narcissist has a catastrophic cost. It's a train wreck waiting to happen. The train will catch up to you, derail your life, and there will be casualties. You'll be left emotionally, physically, and financially annihilated.

PTSD

It's important for family and friends to understand that victims of narcissism or any form of emotional manipulation can experience deep depression, severe anxiety, and/or Post-Traumatic Stress Disorder (PTSD). During my recovery process, I learned from my therapist, my medical physician, and my life coach (a registered nurse) that I had developed PTSD and panic disorder. I'm triggered by seeing handicapped signs, disabled veteran license plates, and wheelchairs. Even the Army logo has given me adverse feelings and negative physical reactions. All of these images remind me of my years of manipulation, betrayal, and the heavy sorrow I carry for a husband I truly believed was handicapped. Being unable to predict when I will be triggered, coupled with chronic anxiety and worrying (which for me causes muscle tension, headaches, and dizziness), has led to regular and frequent panic attacks. Sometimes I can taste the panic in my mouth. Stress hormones lend my saliva a bitter, metallic taste that is very distinct. Thoughts of my experience with Ty literally leave a bad taste in my mouth.

Explaining to a loved one what's happening inside your mind and body can be very difficult. The emotional pain may be so deep it manifests as physical pain. Words of encouragement provide some comfort but cannot change the chemical imbalances that PTSD causes in the brain—imbalances that then force uninvited physical changes to cascade throughout the body. When people say trauma permanently changes you, that's what they mean. It literally changes your body chemistry. There's no such thing as "getting over it," "moving forward," or "leaving the past in the past." Supportive guidance meant to be helpful like "happiness is a choice" is mostly counterproductive. Coaching a victim to choose to be happy only makes them feel more inadequate as they struggle to become "normal" again. PTSD is an emotional monster that hides in the brain like an inoperable tumor. It's not a choice.

PTSD takes many forms and has many causes. It not only afflicts individuals who have experienced violent physical injury or war; it equally impacts people who have lived through emotional, life-changing trauma. PTSD is not a character flaw or a sign of weakness. It's a biological reaction to an intense stressor that thrusts the brain into the fight-or-flight survival mode and leaves it there. Then, when a trigger prompts a connection between the conscious mind and a painful memory, it feels like a wild animal is chasing you and you're running for your life. The nervous system gets stuck in high gear and continuously pumps out stress hormones, causing immense panic. You experience the same level of terror you felt during the inciting event. The mind desperately tries to figure out what happened and scrambles to find a solution so it will never happen again.

If it helps, think of PTSD like an injury, not an illness. Most physical injuries require time to heal. Emotional injuries are the same, only there's no "average timeframe" for healing. Just when you think you're in the clear and back to normal, a trigger will throw the chemicals in your brain off-balance. Then, you're back to the beginning of the healing process all over again. You can ease the symptoms through various methods, but PTSD will always be hiding in the corners of your brain ready to jump out at any time. It hunkers down in the back of the closet waiting to haunt you like a ghost.

Help Yourself

I should note here that my PTSD and panic disorder diagnoses were a long time coming. Perhaps I'm making it sound like they should have been obvious, but they weren't, not to me, not at first. I can't tell you how many specialists I went to thinking something was physically wrong with me. The dizziness, the headaches, the blood vessels bursting in my eyes every few months—these symptoms seemed more in line with a hormonal problem or allergic reaction. So, I had hormone tests and allergy tests. I had MRIs, CT scans, and X-rays. They checked my blood for anomalies and my vision for vertigo. An ENT examined my head to find out why I felt so much pressure and what may be causing the incessant ringing in my ears. A nutritionist examined my diet to make sure there wasn't a nutritional imbalance or deficiency. Finally, and only as a last resort, did I try more therapy, seeking the wisdom of three different counselors and psychiatrists. Collectively, they diagnosed me with an anxiety disorder, a panic disorder, and PTSD. My nervous system was literally on fire!

Although I was extremely hesitant to take any pharmaceutical medications, especially an SSRI, I agreed to try Lexapro. After only a few days on this medication, I started having what's called "brain zaps," like electrical shocks inside your head. Brain zaps more commonly happen to people coming off of antidepressants as opposed to those starting them, but I was the unhappy exception. I immediately stopped taking Lexapro and decided to try some more natural, or you might say unconventional, methods of treatment for easing the debilitating symptoms of PTSD and panic disorder. In no particular order, they were:

- Life coach (Vision boards and journaling)
- Hypnosis (Regression therapy)
- Oils (CBD and essential)
- Emotional Freedom Technique (EFT) tapping
- Positive affirmations
- Hormone Replacement Therapy (HRT)
- Acupuncture
- Massage therapy
- Meditation
- Reiki
- Magnesium baths
- Tibetan singing bowls (Vibration therapy)
- Diet adjustments (no caffeine, no alcohol, no sugar, no gluten)
- Exercise
- Sunshine
- Vitamin supplements for anxiety and brain health

The last "unconventional" method I tried at the advice of my therapist—and it was a scary option for me—was ketamine infusion therapy. Amazingly, it was the only thing that actually helped calm down my nervous system. Today, I'm an advocate and would advise anyone with debilitating anxiety, PTSD, and/or a panic disorder to give supervised ketamine infusion therapy a try. I realize it's expensive and may not be available to everyone, especially if you don't have health insurance. In which case, I'd recommend you do whatever else you can to increase your quality of life while living with PTSD. Lean on those you love, and for goodness sake, do not be ashamed or feel defeated if you need to ask for help, pharmaceutical or otherwise. It's called surviving after being a victim of an emotional manipulator. No one is an island and no one will judge you for trying to take control of your well-being. Fear is not failure and anxiety is not defeat. Help others to help you help yourself. Let them love you. Love is the most profound emotion in life and can heal the deepest of sorrows.

Purpose in the Storm

As my emotional recovery gains more ground, I refuse to be a silent captive of my experiences and censor my voice for behavior that wasn't mine. I no longer have a secret; I have a story. I will not swallow my truth because it's uncomfortable. I didn't lack the courage to live through it, so I won't lack the courage to share it. I will honor the life God gave me and tell my truth, hoping my testimony could be the key that unlocks someone else's prison. If sharing my outlandish journey can shed light on Narcissistic Personality Disorder and Factitious Disorder, be a forewarning, or even provide one single other soul with a sense that they are not alone, then there will be value in telling my story. We've all heard that heartache, suffering, and adversity shape us more profoundly than comfort, stability, and success. Well, consider me shaped—into a megaphone determined to speak for those who are too scared or who cannot speak for themselves.

Before, I was a broken boat without an anchor being tossed around a stormy sea of lies. Ty's turbulent waters were steering me off-course so that the wind of veracity could not fill my sails. The pounding waves against my hull threatened to thrust me overboard. And then, in the distance, the glow of truth. God was the mighty lighthouse that brought me safely to shore. Even though my boat was broken, it had once been a seaworthy vessel and would be again. Until then, I will be a candle in the window of God's lighthouse, signaling to other victims in broken boats. When I repair my damage, I will return to sea in search of other struggling souls. For as I let go of my victimhood, I am changing the meaning of my experience and finding purpose in the storm.

I'm not ashamed to say that I loved Ty with my whole heart. He only loved me with his right side. His left side was a lie.

My Wish for Ty

No matter what you've done, it doesn't disqualify you from God's love. You don't have to earn God's love because you already have it. God will give you all the supply you need. I hope you find your way home. *(John 3:16)*

ACKNOWLEDGMENTS

Thank you to my "elephants"—my son, my family, and friends. You are my favorite people on the planet. You give me purpose and bring me more joy in this life than I thought possible. Without your unconditional love and help, I would have given up long ago.

Thank you to the U.S. Attorney, the federal agents, and the judge who listened to me, believed me, and held Ty legally accountable.

Thank you to my attorney for making my fraudulent marriage evaporate as if it never happened, and for handling all communications between myself and Ty. If I never see or speak to my former husband again it will be too soon.

Thank you to Ty's three boys for accepting me into the family, and to Boerne for accepting me into the community. Walking away without a goodbye may have been the right thing to do, but it was also heart-wrenching. I think of you all often and fondly.

Thank you to Ty's ex-wife for being the boys' solid rock. I admire your strength.

Thank you to the civilian and military doctors who treated Ty when he didn't deserve it.

Thank you to the doctors who treated me when I didn't know what was wrong.

Thank you to the Fisher House Foundation for five months of housing and compassion. My life will be forever humbled after my experience under your comforting roof.

Thank you to my co-workers for being so gracious and understanding. I hope to continue working with you all until we retire.

Last but not least, thank you to my editor, Jessica Bross of Cider Spoon Stories. Your guidance and expertise have been immeasurable. You made my story come to life!

READER RESOURCES

Narcissism:

"Narcissistic Personality Disorder"
https://www.psychologytoday.com/us/conditions/narcissistic-personality-disorder

"Recognizing a Narcissist, with Ramani Durvasula, PhD,"
Speaking of Psychology
https://www.apa.org/research/action/speaking-of-psychology/narcissism.aspx

"Narcissism"
https://www.goodtherapy.org/learn-about-therapy/issues/
narcissism

Factitious Disorder:

"Factitious Disorder"
https://www.mayoclinic.org/diseases-conditions/factitious-
disorder/symptoms-causes/syc-20356028

"Factitious Disorder"
http://www.minddisorders.com/Del-Fi/Factitious-disorder.html

"Factitious Disorders"
https://www.webmd.com/mental-health/factitious-disorders#1

"Patients Who Strive to Be Ill: Factitious Disorder With Physical
Symptoms"
https://ajp.psychiatryonline.org/doi/full/10.1176/appi.
ajp.160.6.1163

Love Bombing:

"Love Bombing: A Narcissist's Secret Weapon"
https://www.psychologytoday.com/us/blog/lifetime-
connections/201804/love-bombing-narcissists-secret-weapon

"How To Spot 'Love Bombing'—A Sneaky Form of Emotional Abuse"
https://www.health.com/relationships/love-bombing-emotional-abuse

"'Love Bombing': What It Is, Why It's Dangerous, and How to Protect Yourself"
https://www.inc.com/justin-bariso/love-bombing-shows-a-twisted-form-of-emotional-intelligence-heres-how-to-protect-yourself.html

"'Love Bombing' Is the Newest Dangerous Dating Trend"
https://nypost.com/2017/08/01/love-bombing-is-the-newest-dangerous-dating-trend/

"Love Bombing: A Seductive & Manipulative Technique"
https://www.elephantjournal.com/2016/01/love-bombing-a-seductive-manipulative-technique/

"Grooming, Manipulation, and Love Bombing"
https://neuroinstincts.com/grooming-manipulation-and-love-bombing/

Supply:

"This Is What Really Makes Narcissists Tick"
https://www.psychologytoday.com/us/blog/evolution-the-self/201507/is-what-really-makes-narcissists-tick

"Narcissism and the Addiction to Narcissistic Supply"
https://narcissisticbehavior.net/narcissism-and-the-addiction-to-
narcissistic-supply/

"Avoid Being a Source of Narcissistic Supply"
https://www.decision-making-confidence.com/narcissistic-
supply.html

Gaslighting:

"How to Tell If Someone Is Gaslighting You"
https://www.newportinstitute.com/resources/mental-health/
what_is_gaslighting_abuse/

"Gaslighting"
https://www.psychologytoday.com/us/basics/gaslighting

"How to Recognize Gaslighting and Get Help"
https://www.healthline.com/health/gaslighting

Mirroring:

"What Is Mirroring and How Do Narcissists Use It to Manipulate
Their Victims?"
https://www.simplypsychology.org/narcissistic-mirroring.html

"Life in the Fun House: Narcissistic Mirroring and Projection"
https://narcissistfamilyfiles.com/2017/10/03/the-narcissists-funhouse-of-mirroring-and-projection/

"If It Seems Too Good to Be True … It Is"
https://narcissistabusesupport.com/red-flags/narcissist-red-flag-mirroring/

Positive Mirroring:

Survive Her Affair by Kevin Jackson
This is a downloadable book:
https://www.goodreads.com/book/show/29216416-survive-her-affair

Losing Yourself:

"How Narcissists Make You Lose Yourself"
https://narcissisms.com/how-narcissists-make-you-lose-yourself/

"Loss of Identity in Narcissistic Relationships: Who Am I?"
https://medium.com/psychology-self-healing/loss-of-identity-in-narcissistic-relationships-who-am-i-23bdbb749678

Books Recommended by My Therapist:

The Sociopath at the Breakfast Table: Recognizing and Dealing With Antisocial and Manipulative People by Jane McGregor, Tim McGregor
https://www.barnesandnoble.com/w/the-sociopath-at-the-breakfast-table-jane-mcgregor/1115532399

The Wizard of Oz and Other Narcissists: Coping with the One-Way Relationship in Work, Love, and Family by Eleanor D. Payson
https://www.goodreads.com/en/book/show/116590

Disarming the Narcissist: Surviving and Thriving with the Self-Absorbed by Wendy T. Behary (Author), Jeffrey Young (Foreword), Daniel J. Siegel MD
https://www.amazon.com/gp/product/B08WHRHCZH/

Rethinking Narcissism: The Secret to Recognizing and Coping with Narcissists by Dr. Craig Malkin
https://www.amazon.com/Rethinking-Narcissism-Secret-Recognizing-Narcissists/dp/0062348116/

Freeing Yourself from the Narcissist in Your Life: At Home. At Work. With Friends. by Linda Martinez-Lewi
https://www.amazon.com/gp/product/0399165770/

WORKS REFERENCED

NPD Statistics references:

"Narcissistic Personality Disorder Causes, Statistics, Signs, Symptoms, & Side Effects"
https://www.addictionhope.com/mood-disorder/narcissistic-personality/

"Narcissism Epidemic: Why There are So Many Narcissists Now"
https://health.usnews.com/health-news/family-health/brain-and-behavior/articles/2009/04/21/narcissism-epidemic-why-there-are-so-many-narcissists-now

"Is Narcissism Common? The Answer May Surprise You"
https://www.sane.org/the-sane-blog/mental-illness/is-narcissism-common-the-answer-may-surprise-you

"How Common Is Narcissistic Abuse in the United States?"
https://psychcentral.com/lib/narcissistic-abuse-affects-over-158-million-people-in-the-u-s/

"Narcissistic Personality Disorder in Clinical Health Psychology Practice: Case Studies of Comorbid Psychological Distress and Life-Limiting Illness" by Elizabeth L. Kacel, Nicolle Ennis, and Deidre B. Pereira
https://www.ncbi.nlm.nih.gov/pmc/articles/PMC5819598/

Factitious Disorder Statistics references:

"Factitious Disorder: A Systematic Review of 455 Cases in the Professional Literature" by Gregory P Yates, M.A., Marc D. Feldman, M.D.
https://www.sciencedirect.com/science/article/pii/S016383431630072X

"A Systematic Review on Factitious Disorders: Psychopathology and Diagnostic Classification"
http://www.jneuropsychiatry.org/peer-review/a-systematic-review-on-factitious-disorders-psychopathology-and-diagnostic-classification.pdf

WORKS REFERENCED

Veteran Suicide Statistics references:

"2022 National Veteran Suicide Prevention Annual Report"
https://www.mentalhealth.va.gov/docs/data-sheets/2022/2022-
National-Veteran-Suicide-Prevention-Annual-Report-
FINAL-508.pdf

"Excess Mortality Rates among Post-9/11 Veterans"
https://www.hsrd.research.va.gov/research/citations/PubBriefs/
articles.cfm?RecordID=1159

Head Injury Deception Statistics references:

"Illness Deception"
https://academic.oup.com/occmed/article/65/7/514/1735283

"Base Rates of Malingering and Symptom Exaggeration"
https://www.tandfonline.com/doi/abs/10.1076/
jcen.24.8.1094.8379

Texas Annulment reference:

"Annulling a Marriage in Texas"
https://texaslawhelp.org/article/annulment-answers-to-common-
questions.

Bowe Bergdahl references:

"Freed War Prisoner Bergdahl Arrives at Army Medical Center in Texas - Pentagon"
https://www.reuters.com/article/us-usa-afghanistan-bergdahl/freed-war-prisoner-bergdahl-arrives-at-army-medical-center-in-texas-pentagon-idINKBN0EO1M620140613

"Bowe Bergdahl Arrives in Texas"
https://www.washingtonpost.com/news/checkpoint/wp/2014/06/12/bowe-bergdahl-set-to-arrive-in-texas-tonight-report-says/

Temporary Duty (TDY) references:

"What Does TDY Stand for in the Military? – Military Jargon Explained"
https://www.thesoldiersproject.org/what-does-tdy-stand-for-in-the-military/

"Temporary Duty Assignments – Understanding Your Pay & Benefits While on TDY Orders"
https://themilitarywallet.com/tdy-orders/

Brook Army Medical Center reference:

https://bamc.tricare.mil/

WORKS REFERENCED

SERE Training references:

"What You Learn at Sere Training"
https://mybaseguide.com/sere-training

"U.S. Army Aviation Center of Excellence and Fort Novosel"
https://home.army.mil/novosel/index.php/tenants/sere

Texas National Guard (SOD-A) – Bee Caves, Texas reference:

"Special Operations Detachment - Africa Crosses One-Year Milestone"
https://www.dvidshub.net/news/117895/special-operations-detachment-africa-crosses-one-year-milestone

INCAP reference:

"Incapacitation of Reserve Component Soldiers"
https://armypubs.army.mil/epubs/DR_pubs/DR_a/ARN30297-AR_135-381-000-WEB-1.pdf

Medical Evaluation Board (MEB) and Physician Evaluation Board (PEB) reference:

https://www.socom.mil/care-coalition/Pages/IDES-Toolkit.aspx

ADA reference:

https://www.ada.gov/

The Fisher House Foundation reference:

https://fisherhouse.org/about/

Center for the Intrepid (CFI) reference:

https://bamc.tricare.mil/Clinics/Center-for-the-Intrepid

Disability Equality Index (DEI) reference:

https://disabilityin.org/what-we-do/disability-equality-index/

Wounded Warrior Project reference:

https://support.woundedwarriorproject.org/

Operation First Response reference:

https://www.operationfirstresponse.org/

Semper Fi Americas Fund reference:

https://thefund.org/

WORKS REFERENCED

Wish For Our Heroes reference:

https://www.wishforourheroes.org/

USO Warrior Family Support Center reference:

https://sanantonio.uso.org/san-antonio-warriorcenter

Special Monthly Compensation Ratings Form 3.350-1:

https://www.ecfr.gov/current/title-38/chapter-I/part-3/subpart-A/
subject-group-ECFR6477ad08d327384/section-3.350

Incapacitation of Reserve Component Soldiers reference:

https://armypubs.army.mil/epubs/DR_pubs/DR_a/ARN30297-
AR_135-381-000-WEB-1.pdf

Functional Neurologic Disorder (FND) reference:

https://www.ninds.nih.gov/health-information/disorders/
functional-neurologic-disorder

Love Hormone (Oxytocin) references:

"The Love Hormone: Oxytocin and Attachment"
https://www.attachmentproject.com/blog/oxytocin-and-attachment/

"Oxytocin: The Love Hormone"
https://www.health.harvard.edu/mind-and-mood/oxytocin-the-love-hormone

Trauma Bond references:

"Trauma Bonds: Breaking the Addiction to Toxic Relationships"
https://katemunden.com/trauma-bonds-breaking-the-addiction-to-toxic-relationships/

"Trauma Bonding Explained: Signs and How to Break the Bond"
https://themendproject.com/trauma-bonding/

"Trauma Bonding, Codependency, and Narcissistic Abuse"
https://www.psychologytoday.com/us/blog/addiction-and-recovery/201905/trauma-bonding-codependency-and-narcissistic-abuse

PTSD references:

"What Is Posttraumatic Stress Disorder (PTSD)?"
https://www.psychiatry.org/patients-families/ptsd/what-is-ptsd

"Posttraumatic Stress Disorder (PTSD)"
https://www.webmd.com/mental-health/post-traumatic-stress-disorder

WORKS REFERENCED

"Posttraumatic Stress Disorder"
https://www.apa.org/topics/ptsd

"Post-traumatic Stress Disorder (PTSD)"
https://www.mayoclinic.org/diseases-conditions/post-traumatic-stress-disorder/symptoms-causes/syc-20355967

"Why PTSD Is a Mental Injury, Not a Mental Illness"
https://www.psychologytoday.com/us/blog/silencing-your-inner-bully/201909/why-ptsd-is-mental-injury-not-mental-illness

"An Injury, Not a Disorder"
https://dartcenter.org/content/injury-not-disorder-0

Panic Disorder references:

"Panic Disorder"
https://www.hopkinsmedicine.org/health/conditions-and-diseases/panic-disorder

"Panic Disorder: When Fear Overwhelms"
https://www.nimh.nih.gov/health/publications/panic-disorder-when-fear-overwhelms

"Panic Attacks and Panic Disorder"
https://www.mayoclinic.org/diseases-conditions/panic-attacks/symptoms-causes/syc-20376021

Taste references:

"Can Anxiety Cause a Metallic Taste in Your Mouth?"
https://www.healthline.com/health/anxiety/metallic-taste-in-mouth-anxiety

"Bad Taste in Mouth Anxiety Symptoms"
https://www.anxietycentre.com/anxiety-disorders/symptoms/bad-taste-in-mouth-anxiety/

"Why Do I Have a Bitter Taste in My Mouth?"
https://www.medicalnewstoday.com/articles/321175#causes

Munchausen Syndrome references:

"Munchausen's Syndrome"
https://www.nhsinform.scot/illnesses-and-conditions/mental-health/munchausens-syndrome

"Baron Münchhausen: History of an Endearing Personage and of a Strange Mental Disorder"
https://pubmed.ncbi.nlm.nih.gov/12422889/

Characteristics of Lying references:

"Nonverbal Signs of Lying"
https://study.com/academy/lesson/nonverbal-signs-of-lying.html

"Just the Bat of an Eye"
https://www.psychologytoday.com/us/blog/let-their-words-do-the-talking/201405/just-the-bat-eye

Narcissism references:

"What Is Narcissist Discard?"
https://www.verywellmind.com/narcissistic-discard-causes-impact-and-coping-strategies-5218979

"The 5 Distinctive Narcissistic Stares and What They Really Mean"
https://medium.com/@dinamin84/the-5-distinctive-narcissistic-stares-and-what-they-really-mean-a28b6f560087

"What Is the Narcissistic Stare? (And 8 More Non-Verbal Signs of a Narcissist)"
https://www.learning-mind.com/narcissistic-stare/

"Is Narcissistic Personality Disorder Inherited or Developed Over Time?"
https://americanbehavioralclinics.com/is-narcissistic-personality-order-inherited-or-developed-over-time/

"What Causes Narcissistic Personality Disorder?"
https://psychcentral.com/disorders/what-causes-narcissistic-personality-disorder

"The Role of Genetics in Narcissistic Personality Disorder"
https://www.verywellmind.com/is-narcissism-genetic-7111210

"How and Why We Lie at Work"
https://hbr.org/2015/01/how-and-why-we-lie-at-work

Department of Justice False Claims Act reference:

https://www.justice.gov/civil/false-claims-act

Department of Veterans Affairs Fraud Claims Form:

https://www.va.gov/COMMUNITYCARE/about_us/POI/poi_
fwa.asp

Social Security Administration Fraud Claims Form:

https://secure.ssa.gov/pfrf/

ABOUT THE AUTHOR

Dee Ashby lives in Austin, Texas. *Left-Side Lie* is her first book.

Made in the USA
Coppell, TX
20 October 2023

23120409R00166